AUSTRALIA

TITLES IN THE MODERN NATIONS OF THE WORLD SERIES INCLUDE:

AUSTRALIA

BY JOHN F. GRABOWSKI

LUCENT BOOKS
SAN DIEGO, CALIFORNIA

THOMSON

GALE

Detroit • New York • San Diego • San Francisco
Boston • New Haven, Conn. • Waterville, Maine
London • Munich

Library of Congress Cataloging-in-Publication Data

Grabowski, John F.
   Australia / by John F. Grabowski.
        p.   cm. — (Modern nations of the world)
Includes bibliographical references and index.
Summary: Discusses Australia's history, geography, government, people,
and culture.
   ISBN 1-56006-566-4 (hardback : alk. paper)
   1. Australia—Juvenile literature.   [1. Australia.]   I. Title.   II. Series.
DU96 .G725   2002
994—dc21

2001006626

Copyright © 2002 by Lucent Books
an imprint of The Gale Group
10911 Technology Place, San Diego, CA 92127

Printed in the U.S.A.

CONTENTS

Introduction

Godzone

Australians sometimes refer to their country as Godzone, or God's Own. To many, this name may seem presumptuous. After visiting this land of warm weather, beautiful beaches, and friendly people, however, it is easy to see how it received this name. Australia is the perfect playground for a fun-loving people who are proud of their country and eager to share its many scenic wonders with visitors.

Australia is an extremely large, sparsely populated island continent located in the Southern Hemisphere. It is home to a variety of plant and animal life found nowhere else in the world. Kangaroos, wombats, platypuses, crocodiles, bandicoots, koalas, emus, and kookaburras patrol the deserts and rain forests, swim the rivers and seas, and glide through the air. Eucalyptus trees, acacia trees, and an abundance of wildflowers decorate the landscape.

The visitor to Australia's shores will find large, sprawling modern cities and colorful sheep stations in the outback; hot, arid deserts and wet, tropical rain forests; a magnificent barrier reef off the coastline and a huge rock in the interior. The nation's myriad wonders, both manufactured and natural, are part of a truly unique environment, one that remains a mystery to many people because of its relative isolation from the rest of the world.

A Clash of Cultures

As a result of its isolation, Australia was the last continent to be settled by Europeans. It was colonized at the end of the eighteenth century by convicts who were sent there from their native England. These British settlers brought their culture and customs along with them. What they found was a group of people who could not have been more unlike them.

Australia was home to Aboriginals who had occupied the land for some fifty thousand years. Their hunter-gatherer lifestyle was completely foreign to the Europeans. The scantily clad nomads lived peacefully on the land, worshipped ancestors, and survived on a strange diet of seeds, animals, and insects. It is not surprising that the two cultures soon clashed, leading to fighting and bloodshed. It would take years for them to begin to understand and accept each other. This process is ongoing and is still not complete.

A MULTICULTURAL SOCIETY

Over the past fifty years, Australia has become recognized as one of the most successful nations in building a culturally diverse society. Until the twentieth century, the majority of the Europeans who lived there were of British descent. Since then, a multitude of different ethnic groups have been added to the Australian mix. Immigrants came to the new land in search of gold in the 1850s and in search of new opportunities after the two world wars. In addition, since 1945, thousands have come to Australia to escape persecution in other countries. Today, nearly one out of every four Australians was born overseas, and more than one-quarter of the population

The outback, one of Australia's many unique geographical regions, provides ideal conditions for raising sheep.

Australians are fervent sports fans. Here, children wave the national flag at a cricket match.

has at least one parent who was born outside of the country. People from more than 160 foreign nations have chosen to become Australian citizens.

The most recent wave of immigrants has come from Australia's Asian neighbors. These people have added a new layer to the rich mosaic that is the nation's multicultural society. Many have joined ethnic communities where their languages and customs have been preserved.

THE AUSTRALIAN PERSONALITY

Many of the characteristics of the Australian national identity have been carried down through the years by descendants of the first settlers. Those colonists had to be courageous and resourceful to settle the continent. They could not rely on outside help for the supplies they needed to survive. Their survival in a harsh environment depended on their independence and initiative. They were on their own in a strange land, thousands of miles from their place of birth.

The nation's isolation also allowed the colonists to do things at their own pace. This has resulted in a national character that is relaxed and places more emphasis on contentment than on success. Australians are dedicated to enjoying life. They fill their leisure time with activities that take advantage of their country's warm weather and scenic beauty. Sports are a national passion, and Australians enjoy a wide range of them as both participants and spectators.

Among the most endearing characteristics of the Australian personality are friendliness, loyalty, and a sense of humor. As former prime minister Robert Hawke once said of his fellow citizens, "They're very friendly people, people not prone to, as we say 'dip your lid,' to others in a sense of recognizing a superiority in one class of people. There is a phrase we have in Australia—the 'fair go.' The fair go really means that all people are created with the right to develop and express themselves."[1] Australians don't take themselves too seriously, and enjoy poking fun at those who do. This irreverence is in stark contrast to the traditional reserve that their British ancestors exhibited.

Loyal friends were a necessity for the early settlers. If people worked together, their chances for survival increased. Today, this "mateship" continues to be important. To an Aussie, a mate is not a husband or wife, but rather a special friend who can be counted on to be there in good times and in bad. They are willing to accept people for who they are, not what they have.

Things were not always so, however. Fear of losing jobs to immigrants from neighboring Asian countries and the desire to keep Australia overwhelmingly Caucasian led to the Immigration Restrictions Act of 1901. This was the basis for the unofficial "white Australia policy" that remained in force until the 1960s. Today, however, the nation has moved away from its decidedly British heritage and evolved into a country with a rich cultural blend. No matter what Australians' ethnicity may be, they all share a love of their land, its magnificent climate, and its sense of friendship toward all. To them, Australia truly is Godzone.

THE LAND DOWN UNDER

As an island continent, Australia has been isolated from every one of the world's other large landmasses for some 50 million years. Because of this, life forms that have developed over the centuries evolved in response to local conditions, independent of developments elsewhere. The result is a distinct array of plants and animals not found anywhere else in the world, existing in a strange and forbidding landscape.

THE ISLAND CONTINENT

Most modern scientists believe that 250 million years ago, all the land on Earth formed one large supercontinent called Pangaea (Greek for "all the Earth"). Eventually, this giant landmass split in two: a northern part—Laurasia—and a southern part—Gondwana. Approximately 100 million years ago, Gondwana itself broke apart into the various southern continents. Australia and Antarctica remained attached until 50 million years later. At that time, Australia separated and began moving northward toward the equator.

The enormous island of Australia—at just under 3 million square miles, it is the sixth largest country in the world—is nearly the size of the continental United States, but with just 7 percent of the U.S.'s population. It lies between the Pacific and Indian Oceans in the Southern Hemisphere. The Timor and Arafura Seas separate it from Indonesia in the northwest, while in the northeast, Torres Strait separates it from Papua New Guinea. The Coral Sea Islands lie to the northeast in the Coral Sea, with New Zealand across the Tasman Sea in the southeast. To the south, the Indian Ocean comes between Australia and Antarctica. Because of its position in the Southern Hemisphere, Australia is often called "the Land Down Under."

STATES AND TERRITORIES

The Commonwealth of Australia is composed of six self-governing states and two mainland territories. Western Australia, the largest state in area, occupies the western third of the continent. In the central region, South Australia lies south of the Northern Territory. Moving from north to south, Queensland, New South Wales, and Victoria make up the eastern part of the country. The Australian Capital Territory (ACT), located within New South Wales, is the home of Canberra, the national capital. The island state of Tasmania, smallest of the six states, lies south of Victoria, across Bass Strait.

In addition to the states and mainland territories, Australia also administers seven other territories. These are Norfolk Island and the uninhabited Coral Sea Islands Territory to the east; Christmas Island, the Cocos (Keeling) Islands, and the uninhabited Ashmore and Cartier Islands Territory to the northwest; and the Australian Antarctic Territory and the sub-Antarctic territory of Heard Island and the McDonald Islands to the south.

GEOGRAPHIC REGIONS

Australia is one of the oldest, driest, and flattest of the world's seven continents. It is divided into several geographic regions, beginning in the west with the Western Plateau. The plateau, which covers almost two-thirds of the country, is a flat, low-lying area that receives a minimal amount of rainfall. The Great Sandy, Gibson, Great Victoria, and Tamani Deserts are found here. The interior region of the country, often referred to as the outback, is sparsely inhabited. Much of the land takes on a reddish hue because of the presence of iron in the soil. Because of this, the geographic center of the country near Alice Springs is commonly known as the Red Center.

The Western Plateau gradually merges with the Central Plains or Central Lowlands. This area also receives little rain, but cattle ranchers graze their animals on the grass and shrubs. Rivers and lakes dot the area, but they are usually dry. Sometimes the rivers leave behind small ponds when they dry up. These ponds, called billabongs, were made famous in the popular Australian folk song "Waltzing Matilda." The dry white bed of a salt lake—called a playa—might stretch for miles and miles. Lake Eyre, Australia's lowest point at fifty-two feet below sea level, is one such lake. It may fill with water only one or two times in a century.

Moving east, the Central Plains give way to the Eastern Highlands. This ridge of hills and mountains is also called the Great Dividing Range. Australia's highest mountains, the Australian Alps, are located at the southern end of the range. Mount Kosciusko, at 7,310 feet, is the continent's highest peak. The nation's two longest rivers—the Murray and the Darling—have their sources in the highlands. They flow westward until they merge, and eventually empty into the Great Australian Bight near Adelaide.

To the east of the mountains is the Eastern Lowland, a narrow strip of land along the coast. The region contains the county's best farmland and the greatest concentration of population. Some of the area is heavily forested, but much has been cleared as the cities have expanded.

The northernmost region of the country, known as the Top End, is in the tropical monsoon belt. Much of this area in Arnhem Land, around the Gulf of Carpentaria, contains lush forests and teems with wildlife. Kakadu National Park, with its stunning scenic beauty, is one of Australia's most extraor-

This unusual rock formation stands in a grove of trees at Kakadu National Park in northern Australia.

dinary locations. Not far to the east lies one of the world's great natural wonders, the Great Barrier Reef.

THE GREAT BARRIER REEF

Author Elspeth Huxley asks, "How can you convey the dreamlike fantasy of an undersea forest of seaweed or garden of anemones, the incredible population of tropical fishes, the coral-encrusted clams?"[2] The fantasy she refers to is not a dream at all, but rather a structure that lies off the coast of Queensland, in the northeast corner of the continent. It is the Great Barrier Reef, the world's largest living organism and one of Australia's main tourist attractions. The spectacular 1,250-mile-long multicolored structure is actually a system of some 2,600 reefs extending northward from Bundaberg to the tip of Cape York. It was formed over the course of thousands of years by a buildup of billions of creatures called coral polyps. As the tiny animals died, their limestone skeletons remained. New polyps grew on top of the old, eventually forming "walls" that stretch along the continental shelf.

The reef is home to a wide variety of animal life. Approximately 1,500 species of fish, 4,000 kinds of mollusks, and 350 echinoderms (starfish, sea urchins, and sea cucumbers) call the reef home. Some 240 species of birds breed and raise their young there.

One of the region's most spectacular events occurs for a few nights every year. At that time, the polyps reproduce, and

The Great Barrier Reef is the world's largest coral formation and one of Australia's top tourist attractions.

billions of eggs and sperm fill the waters. The sight has been compared to an underwater snowstorm. This phenomenon occurs in October or November, in the middle of the Australian spring.

A HARSH CLIMATE

Because of its location in the Southern Hemisphere, Australia's seasons are the exact opposite of those in North America and Europe. Spring begins in September, summer in December, autumn in March, and winter in June. As a result, it is not unusual to find many Australians spending Christmas at the beach.

CYCLONE TRACY

The most devastating natural disaster to hit Australia occurred on Christmas Eve 1974. On that date, the city of Darwin in the Northern Territory was hit by Cyclone Tracy, with winds estimated at over 150 miles per hour. By the time the storm swept back out to sea, it had killed sixty-five people, caused an estimated $650 million in damages, and destroyed approximately 70 percent of the city's homes.

Tracy came into existence on December 20 as a weak tropical depression about 450 miles northeast of Darwin in the Arafura Sea. The winds intensified over the next twenty-four hours, and the storm's status was upgraded to that of a cyclone. It slowly moved southwest and appeared to be a small threat to the Australian mainland. However, after passing the western tip of Bathurst Island, Tracy turned around and began accelerating toward the city. The first winds arrived at 10 P.M. on the twenty-fourth, but the brunt of the storm was not felt until early Christmas morning.

When its radio transmitters were damaged, the city lost contact with the outside world for several hours. By the time news of the disaster finally reached the southern states, the city had been leveled. Essential services such as power, water, sewerage, and communications had been severed. With the risk of disease a serious threat, more than half of Darwin's population of forty-eight thousand was evacuated. The damage to Darwin was so great, most of the city had to be completely rebuilt over the succeeding years.

Displaced Darwin residents survey the damage caused by Cyclone Tracy in 1974.

Most of the continent is warm and dry, and the southern region is the coolest. In parts of the Australian Alps, snow covers the peaks in winter. In the interior, temperatures may reach well above one hundred degrees Fahrenheit in the daytime, then fall drastically at night. Much of the outback gets no rain at all for most of the year.

In the Top End, there are just two seasons: the wet and the dry. The wet season drenches the land with monsoon rains. Occasionally, tropical cyclones may hit the coast and do extensive damage with their torrential rains and terrifying winds as Cyclone Tracy did to Darwin in 1974. The temperatures in the north are warm year-round, giving rise to the region's nickname, "Land of Two Summers."

A DIVERSITY OF FLORA

Australia's mostly arid climate and relative isolation provided many surprises for the Europeans who first visited its shores. When British captain James Cook sailed the *Endeavour* along the eastern coast of Australia in April 1770, he was

AUSTRALIA'S WORLD HERITAGE AREAS

In 1972, the United Nations Educational, Scientific, and Cultural Organization (UNESCO) adopted the World Heritage Convention to protect areas of universal natural and cultural significance. Currently, fourteen sites in Australia are on the World Heritage List, chosen for their natural, historic, or archaeological value. These sites include Shark Bay, the Tasmanian Wilderness, Kakadu National Park, Lord Howe Island, and the Central Eastern Rainforest Reserves of Australia.

In addition to being home to a large colony of marine fauna, Shark Bay's algae-covered rocks (stromatolites) are the oldest form of life known on Earth. The Tasmanian Wilderness, covering approximately 20 percent of the island of Tasmania, is Australia's largest conservation zone. Kakadu National Park is a huge region of exceptional beauty containing a wealth of archaeological and rock art sites. The natural beauty of crescent-shaped Lord Howe Island has led many to refer to it as paradise on earth. Four major types of rain forest—subtropical, dry, warm temperate, and cool temperate—are found in the Central Eastern Rainforest Reserves of Australia.

accompanied by Sir Joseph Banks, a renowned botanist. The bay they entered was originally named Stingray Harbour. Because of the wide array of strange and exotic plants Banks found and collected there, however, it was renamed Botany Bay. More than twenty thousand species of plants occur there naturally.

Because of the continent's 50 million years of isolation, most of the varieties of plant life that delighted Banks were unique, found nowhere else in the world. These included more than 550 species of eucalypts (or gum trees) and close to 800 species of acacia (or wattle trees). The eucalypts, Australia's most common trees, dominate the forested and better-watered regions of the country, particularly in the east and southwest. The leaves of the tree contain a fragrant oil that is used for medicinal purposes. The mountain ash (*Eucalyptus regnans*) is the tallest flowering plant in the world, occasionally reaching heights of more than three hundred feet. Much of the southern outback is covered by eucalypt mallee scrubs (stunted trees or shrubs).

This forest in Victoria is dominated by Australia's most common tree, the eucalyptus.

Acacias are most prevalent in the drier, semi-arid regions. Their yellow flowers can be seen throughout the country. The golden wattle is the unofficial national floral emblem of Australia. People are encouraged to plant acacia trees on September 1, which is National Wattles Day.

To survive and flourish, Australia's flora have had to adapt to the continent's harsh climate and environment. An example of such a plant is the spinifex grass that covers much of the desert plains. Because of the brutal heat in the country's interior, fires are a constant threat. Spinifex plants will only germinate in the presence of nutrients that become available after a fire burns.

The seeds of some plants lie dormant in the soil for years at a time. When a rare rainfall washes the area, colorful flowers appear for a period of one or two months. The colors attract birds and insects, which then pollinate the flowering plants. Other plants attract particular species with their nectars, or by their unusual shapes that are designed to scrape against birds or insects as they feed.

NATIVE ANIMALS

Australian fauna are as unusual as the environment in which they live. Mammals are particularly distinctive because many are scarce or nonexistent anywhere else. These include the monotremes, or egg-laying mammals. Monotremes' evolutionary lineage can be traced back almost 200 million years. Often regarded as living fossils, the only ones that exist today are the platypus and two varieties of echidna, or spiny anteaters. They are found only in Australia and nearby New Guinea.

More than half of the mammals native to Australia are *marsupials,* or animals that develop their young in a pouch (the word *marsupial* comes from the Latin word *marsupium,* meaning pouch or purse). Unquestionably the most popular is the kangaroo, of which there are approximately fifty species found in Australia. Kangaroos range in size from the two-inch-high dusky hopping mouse to the red kangaroo, which grows to heights of more than six feet. According to legend, the word *kangaroo* is an Aboriginal term meaning "I don't understand you." On his trip to Australia in 1770, Captain James Cook supposedly came across one of the creatures and asked a native what it was called. When the Aborigine replied, "Kangaroo," Cook assumed that was the animal's name.

Although some smaller roos climb trees in the rain forests like monkeys, the variety most people are familiar with travels in herds, hopping across the bushlands and desert. Their powerful hind legs allow them to move at speeds up to forty miles per hour, and to jump nearly thirty feet. They are able to live in the desert because they need little water to survive. Although fur usually prevents heat from escaping, in the case of the kangaroo, it helps to keep heat out. In addition, by licking its forearms, the animal loses heat through evaporation.

Another animal native to Australia is the koala. Although it looks like a cuddly teddy bear, appearances are deceiving. It is not a bear at all, but rather a marsupial that spends most of its life in trees. It sleeps up to twenty hours a day and rarely

Australia is home to approximately fifty species of kangaroos, which range in height from two inches to more than six feet.

THE PLATYPUS

Australia is home to many unusual animals, one of which is the platypus (*Ornithorhynchus anatinus*). The first one to be seen by Europeans was observed near the Hawkesbury River in 1797. The next year, the dried skin of one was sent to Britain for study. Scientists claimed it was a fake, believing it to be the body of a rabbit with a duck's beak and feet grafted on. It would be five years before the animal's existence was established beyond doubt.

The platypus is a semiaquatic egg-laying mammal (monotreme) that is the size of a small cat. It has a fur-covered body with a broad, flat tail, and a bill and webbed feet like a duck. Although it lays eggs like a bird, it carries its young in a pouch under its belly. The babies are nourished by their mother's milk, which oozes out onto a patch of fur.

Although the platypus has keen sight on land, its eyes are covered when it swims. Until recent times, it was thought the animal just swam along near the river bottom, grabbing whatever food it happened to blunder into. Now, however, scientists have discovered it employs an unusual "sixth sense." The bill contains fine nerve receptors that can pick up weak electric fields given off by shrimp and tiny insects. It can even sense prey that is hidden under rocks and mud.

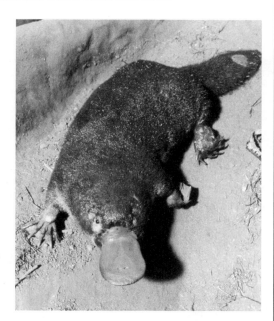

The platypus is unique as one of only two species of mammals that lay eggs.

drinks water. (Its name, in fact, is an Aboriginal word meaning "no water.") Instead, it lives off the leaves of the eucalyptus tree, but only of the variety in which it was born. Koalas were prized for their soft fur and were almost hunted to extinction. Today, trapping koalas is illegal, but their population is still small.

Wombats are still another species of marsupial that calls Australia home. These burrowing creatures weigh anywhere from sixty to one hundred pounds and come out of their holes only at night. Thousands of years ago, ancestors of these animals grew to be the size of cows. Because of the way their bodies have adapted to the warm climate, wombats can survive for years without taking a single drink of water.

Although the koala resembles a bear, it is actually a marsupial that develops its offspring in a pouch.

THE DINGO FENCE

Australia is the site of the longest manufactured structure in the world. More than twice the length of the Great Wall of China, the 3,300-mile-long Dingo Fence stretches from Queensland (where it is called the Barrier Fence), through New South Wales (Border Fence), and finally, to South Australia (Dog Fence). The entire configuration is known as the Dingo Fence. The fence was originally begun in the 1880s to keep rabbits out of the pasture lands used by sheep. Although it failed to do so, it did prevent larger animals from getting in.

The fence was rebuilt in the 1920s to protect sheep from the vicious wild dingoes that roamed the countryside. Completed in 1960, the six-foot-high structure consists of a wide mesh at the top, which prevents dingoes from jumping over it. The smaller mesh of the lower portion is designed to keep out smaller animals such as foxes. In some areas, electrified wire, poison, and traps also help the fence do its job. Unfortunately, while solving one problem, the Dingo Fence has introduced another. Because of the absence of predators on the sheep-farming side of the fence, the kangaroo population has increased tremendously. The two groups of animals are now in competition for the precious water and grass necessary for the sheep's survival.

Perhaps the most vicious marsupial is the small, black Tasmanian devil. This remarkable creature the size of a small dog has powerful jaws and sharp teeth that allow it to eat almost anything. Now found only in Tasmania, the devil is a carnivorous (flesh-eating) scavenger that devours its prey—fur, bones, and all. It was named by early European settlers because of its bone-chilling screech.

Dingoes are wild dogs that are believed to have been brought to Australia by the Aborigines when they migrated from Asia thousands of years ago. The animals are vicious predators and attack sheep, cattle, kangaroos, and, some claim, even people. In a famous 1982 court case, Lindy Chamberlain was convicted of murdering her one-month-old daughter, Azaria. She claimed the baby had been carried off by a dingo near Ayers Rock. Four years later, the child's bloody jacket was found near the rock, and Chamberlain's conviction was overturned. The story was later made into the movie *A Cry in the Dark,* starring Meryl Streep.

Other animals introduced to Australia over the years are rabbits, foxes, cows, water buffalo, sheep, pigs, and even camels. Australia's population of free-ranging camels is the largest in the world. They were originally brought in to help explorers traverse the thousands of square miles of desert.

IN THE WATER

More than five hundred species of lizards and snakes populate the continent. Among the most dangerous are two varieties of crocodile found in the Top End: saltwater (salties) and freshwater (freshies). The large, more vicious salties have rounded snouts, while the freshies' are narrower. Salties are known to attack human beings, cattle, and freshies. The flesh-eating salties may grow to fifteen feet in length, while their freshwater kin, who survive on fish, plants, and small animals, measure approximately eight feet in length.

The length of these reptiles, however, pales in comparison to that of the python, Australia's largest snake, which sometimes reaches twenty-five feet. The deadly python coils its body around its victims and squeezes them to death. It then swallows its prey whole.

Perhaps the most unusual of Australia's reptiles is the frilled lizard. When frightened, the frilled lizard unfurls its wide, fanlike

When threatened, the frilled lizard ruffles out its colorful frill like an open umbrella.

collar, then runs away on its two hind legs. Despite its scary appearance, the lizard is in reality quite harmless.

IN THE AIR

The continent of Australia is also home to more than seven hundred species of birds. The largest of these is the giant, flightless emu, second in size among birds only to the ostrich. The friendly emus usually roam the countryside in pairs, supporting their fat bodies on long, thin legs. Their large, dark green eggs are prized by the Aborigines, who decorate them and sell them as souvenirs.

The kookaburra, sometimes called the "laughing jackass" because of its noisy cackle, is another bird unique to Australia. So, too, are the cassowary, galah, fairy penguin, lily walker, and lyrebird. They share their homeland with a variety of parrots, cockatoos, budgerigars, finches, rainbow lorikeets, and numerous others. The result is a colorful array of bird life which, when combined with the other fauna and flora of the continent, helps make Australia a naturalist's delight.

THE FIRST AUSTRALIANS

It is fitting that a land sometimes referred to as the oldest continent is also home to what is recognized as the world's oldest culture. Australian Aborigines have inhabited the land for more than fifty thousand years. As primitive as their culture may be, it has proved resilient enough to overcome the obstacles presented by a harsh environment and to survive the arrival of the Europeans just over two hundred years ago.

HUNTER-GATHERERS IN HARMONY WITH THE LAND

Hunter-gatherers were members of early societies who subsisted on food obtained by hunting and foraging. Some primitive groups, including the Aboriginals of Australia, continue to use these methods today to live in harmony with the land and with each other.

As far as anyone knows, there was never a single, unified Aboriginal nation on the continent. The five hundred or so Aboriginal tribes, or nations, learned to live in harmony with the hot, dry land. Each had its own territory and language. Tribes were composed of smaller groups called clans, and these, in turn, of families. Most of the families' time and energy was spent gathering or searching for food. (Because of this, they had little use for material possessions, which only served to slow them down in their nomadic travels.) Finding plants to use for food and medicine was primarily the work of the women. The men and boys hunted large game, which was then butchered and distributed to all members of the tribe. Fruits, berries, and root vegetables, such as wild yams, could be found in the forested regions. In the deserts, the seeds of the various grasses were ground up and used to make a kind of bread. If plants were harvested, seed was spread to ensure that new ones took their place.

25

Aborigines, who have inhabited Australia for more than fifty thousand years, are recognized as the world's oldest culture.

Aboriginals were sometimes referred to as fire-stick farmers. Fire was used as a tool to help them make better use of the land. Among other things, it helped kill weeds that threatened to strangle trees, scared off animals that might eat their food, and helped some plants to grow by replacing needed nutrients in the soil.

When possible, Aboriginals hunted animals like the wombat, wallaby, bandicoot, and kangaroo. They generally hurled spears at their prey, often with the aid of a *woomera,* or spear-thrower. They might track an animal for hours, remaining motionless for long periods until their quarry let down its guard. At other times, hunters worked in teams, driving an animal toward another hunter or into an enclosure where it could be captured.

Another tool used for hunting was the boomerang. The boomerang westerners are most familiar with is a curved stick which, when thrown, returns to the thrower. Other types, however, were not designed to come back. This variety of hunting club was thrown at the feet of an animal, disabling and snaring it.

Fishing was an important activity for families that lived near coastlines or rivers. Shellfish, turtles, seals, and an occasional beached whale were enjoyed when available. The men used spears and nets to gather their catches, and sometimes fished from rafts made out of logs.

Since plants and animals were not overly abundant in the outback, other sources of food had to be found. Insects of various kinds came to be an important part of the Aboriginal diet, and continue to be so today. Two of the most popular insects are the honey ant and the witchetty grub. Honey ants collect nectar from plants, but rather than store it in combs like bees, they store it in the swollen bodies of worker ants called repletes. The other ants feed off the honey when nourishment is needed. Aboriginals bite off the grape-sized bulbs to enjoy the sweet, tangy liquid.

The witchetty grub is another Aboriginal delicacy. It is found in the roots of the mulga tree and acacia bushes. The white caterpillars are the size of a small carrot. They are eaten raw, or chopped up and roasted in ashes.

According to Aboriginal beliefs, the plants, animals, fish, and insects were provided to them by the ancestors. These objects came into existence many centuries ago in a period known as the Dreamtime. This period is the basis for all Aboriginal philosophy and religion.

AN ANCIENT JOURNEY

During the last ice age, sea levels around the world were much lower than they are today. Land that is currently submerged was above water, including a strip connecting Australia and New Guinea. The ancestors of Australia's Aborigines (a name meaning "first ones," given to them by the Europeans in the late eighteenth century) arrived from Southeast Asia over similar land bridges and short stretches of sea. When the polar ice caps began to melt, the level of the waters rose some five hundred or more feet. The result was the isolation of the continent and its inhabitants from the rest of the world.

Descriptions of journeys from faraway lands are part of many Aboriginal legends. One such trip is described by Wandjuk Marika in Stuart Macintyre's *A Concise History of Australia:*

"The truth is, of course, that my own people, the Riratjungi, are descended from the great Djankawa who came from the island of Baralku, far across the sea. Our spirits return to Baralku when we die. Djankawa came in his canoe with his two sisters, following the morning star which guided them to the shores of Yelangbara on the eastern coast of Arnhem Land."

The honey ant, which stores plant nectar in its swollen body, is an important part of the Aboriginal diet.

ABORIGINAL PHILOSOPHY AND RELIGION

Aboriginals see themselves as one with nature. All things on Earth are viewed as part human and vice versa. Those who live in a particular area are, in fact, one with the land. If the land is destroyed or desecrated, so, too, are the natives. When an Aboriginal dies, some part of his being survives and returns to the place in the earth from where it came.

The Aboriginals call the period when the physical world was created the Dreamtime. Prior to that, there was just a flat emptiness, with no form or shape. In the Dreamtime, the Aboriginals' spiritual ancestors rose from beneath the ground to form the mountains and rivers, flora and fauna. Finally, they made human beings and established the rules that regulate Aboriginal society. After all had been created, the ancestors returned to the ground. They remain there to the present day in the Dreaming, which goes on forever.

The legends of these ancestors are kept alive from generation to generation through stories and ceremonies. Each Dreamtime story concerns a specific part of the landscape. The landscapes join with one another to form a "track" called a Songline. The Songlines intersect with each other across the continent, enabling Aboriginal tribes to relate to each other.

Songs and dances also help the Aboriginals communicate with their ancestors. Music often accompanies the songs. The most common instrument used is the *didgeridoo,* which is a long, hollow wind instrument that emits a low, deep sound.

Some of the more elaborate dances are part of religious ceremonies. Attendance at the most secret of these is limited to adult males of the tribe. In these rites, the Aboriginals call upon the power of the ancestors to help plants and animals to grow, and to help maintain life along its proper course.

The only outsiders who interfered with this "proper course" were occasional Papuans from across the Torres Strait in the northwest, and Macassans from an island in what is now known as Indonesia. These traders and fishermen often stayed for several months before returning to their homes with tortoise shell, sandalwood, and a kind of sea cucumber called trepang, which was a popular food in the Orient. Although fights occasionally occurred, relations with the Macassans were generally friendly. This limited contact with outsiders did not prepare the Aboriginals for the arrival of the first Europeans that visited the continent.

THE FIRST EUROPEANS

As early as A.D. 150, Ptolemy, the Greek astronomer, mathematician, and geographer, speculated on the existence of a large landmass in the Southern Hemisphere. This *terra*

An Aborigine plays the didgeridoo, a long wooden instrument that produces a low-pitched sound.

australis incognita (unknown southern land) had to exist, he reasoned, to counterbalance the large landmasses of the Northern Hemisphere. Without it, the top-heavy world would not be able to spin on its axis. Some went so far as to hypothesize the existence of "antipodes," a race of men whose feet faced backward.

Such a land remained just a theory until the sixteenth century. Although early Portuguese explorers told of coming across a mysterious southern land on their trips to South America, no land was definitely identified. However, a series of maps drawn in Dieppe, France, between 1540 and 1566 show a large mass identified as Java la Grande lying southwest of Indonesia.

It was not until the early seventeenth century, when Holland had become a trading force in the East Indies, that Eu-

THE MAHOGANY SHIP

In 1836, a whaling ship was wrecked at the mouth of the Hopkins River near Warrnambool on the southwest coast of Victoria. The three survivors of the disaster began walking back along the shoreline to the whaling station located on Griffith Island at Port Fairy. During their trek, they stumbled across the remains of an old shipwreck at the mouth of the Merri River. The condition of the ship suggested it had been there as long as two hundred years. More than thirty other sightings of the wreck were reported over the next half century. The ship became known as the Mahogany Ship because of its dark-colored timbers.

As time passed, the wreck was buried beneath the shifting sands. Many searched for the wreck in the intervening years, but without success. In July 1999, interest in the Mahogany Ship was renewed when a sample of wood was discovered that was believed to have possibly come from the ship.

The ship is thought to have been the remains of a Portuguese caravel (a small, light sailing vessel) sent to explore the east coast of Australia in 1522. If it indeed was Portuguese, it would mean that Europeans visited Australia's east coast more than two centuries before Captain James Cook. It would also explain a mysterious series of maps made by cartographers (mapmakers) in the French town of Dieppe in the mid-sixteenth century, maps that show a land discovered by the Portuguese that was the size and location of Australia.

ropeans are known to have set foot on Australia. The first was Willem Jansz, who reached the western shore of the Cape York Peninsula in 1606, sailing from Java on the *Duyfken* (Little Dove) in search of New Guinea. Finding the land barren and the natives unfriendly, Jansz remained only a short time. As was noted in the books of the East India Company, there was "no good to be done there."[3]

Five years later, Dutch explorer Dirck Hartog, commander of the *Eendracht,* landed at Shark Bay off the coast of western Australia when his boat was blown off course en route to the East Indies. While there, he nailed a pewter plate from the ship, inscribed with a record of his visit, to a pole. The plate was found in 1697 by another Dutch navigator, Willem de Vlamingh. It now resides in the Rijksmuseum in Amsterdam.

Dutch explorer and navigator Abel Tasman.

Following Hartog's voyage, other explorers were blown off course and touched on the great South Land. The Dutch East India Company became more and more interested in the region and decided to finance a lengthy expedition to explore it and search for trade opportunities. They sent out Abel Tasman, who mapped large parts of Australia and New Zealand between 1642 and 1644. Off the southern coast of the continent, he navigated the coast of an island he named Van Diemen's Land after the governor-general of the East Indies, Antonij Van Diemen. More than two centuries later, it was renamed Tasmania in Tasman's honor.

The British did not set foot on the continent until 1688, and then only briefly. William Dampier was an English adventurer and buccaneer. As a crew member on the pirate ship *Cygnet,* he had a chance to explore the northwest coast of Australia— or New Holland as it had become known—when his ship spent three months there while undergoing repairs. He eventually returned to England and recounted his experiences in a book entitled *New Voyage Around the World.* Dampier made one other trip to New Holland. It would be the better part of a century before the British decided to explore further.

CAPTAIN JAMES COOK

By the middle of the eighteenth century, England had taken its place as the world's leading maritime nation. In 1768, Captain James Cook was put in command of a scientific expedition to Tahiti to study the path of the planet Venus as it crossed the Sun. From there he was to continue on to the South Pacific to look for the Great South Land.

Sailing aboard the *Endeavour,* Cook reached the east coast of Australia on April 28, 1770. The ship sailed into a body of water just south of present-day Sydney. Cook named it Botany Bay because of the many varieties of fauna found in the region. The *Endeavour* continued northward charting the coast. It was wrecked on the Great Barrier Reef, but continued on after repairs were made. Before heading back home, he reached what is now Possession Island in Torres Strait off the tip of the Cape York Peninsula. There, Cook claimed the entire eastern half of the continent for King George III and called it New South Wales.

Cook returned to New South Wales aboard the *Resolution* in a voyage begun in 1772. On this trip, he covered large areas of the South Pacific. In doing so, he proved once and for all that there was no Great South Land. The only inhabited continent in that part of the world was New South Wales. It would not be long before the British found a use for the land Cook had claimed for the throne.

A USE FOR THE NEW LAND

Meanwhile, mid-eighteenth-century England was experiencing dire social problems. Unemployment in London was widespread, and people in the slums faced horrible living conditions. Crime was rampant, as many resorted to stealing to obtain food for themselves and their families. To combat these problems, laws were passed assessing severe jail sentences for even minor offenses. The result was jails that were overflowing with convicts.

To alleviate the overcrowding, many prisoners were shipped off to British colonies, where they toiled as laborers to work off their sentences. This practice was known as transportation. The American colonies were one of the main locales used in this way. After they declared their independence from England in 1776, however, they could no longer be used for this purpose. As a temporary solution, many con-

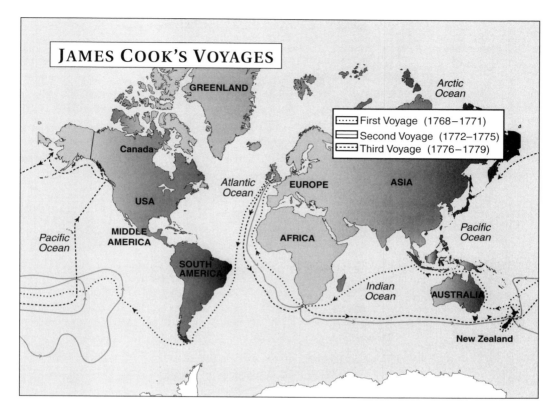

JAMES COOK'S VOYAGES

First Voyage (1768–1771)
Second Voyage (1772–1775)
Third Voyage (1776–1779)

victs were housed in the rotted hulks of old ships along the Thames River and in several southern ports. In searching for another region that could be used as a penal colony (a place for the punishment of criminals), British eyes turned toward New South Wales.

ARRIVAL OF THE FIRST FLEET

Australia appeared to be the ideal solution to England's problem. The area around Botany Bay was first suggested as a possible site for a penal colony by Sir Joseph Banks, the botanist who had accompanied James Cook on his 1770 voyage. He described the land's resources as adequate: "The proportion of rich soil was small in comparison to the barren, but sufficient to support a very large number of people. . . . The country was well supplied with water. There were no beasts of prey."[4]

The decision was made, and in August 1786, Captain Arthur Phillip was appointed commander of what would come to be known as the First Fleet. On May 13, 1787, he set sail from Portsmouth on the fourteen-thousand-mile voyage with eleven ships—six transports, three storeships, and two warships. Almost 1,400 people made the trip, 784 of them convicts (including 191 female convicts who were transported along with 13 of their children). Eight months later, they arrived at Botany Bay. The fleet remained there just a brief period of time, however, since there was little fresh water available and no place where ships could anchor close to shore. (Banks had visited the land in late autumn. When the First Fleet arrived, it was the middle of summer and conditions were much less favorable.) The ships continued further north and arrived at Port Jackson (Sydney Harbour) on January 26, 1788. This new location better suited Phillip and the fleet. As he later recounted, "We got into Port Jackson in the afternoon and had the satisfaction of finding the finest harbour in the world, in which a thousand sail of the line may ride in the most perfect security."[5]

THE FIRST SETTLEMENT

Most of the prisoners who were transported to Australia had been convicted of minor offenses in England. They had received sentences averaging seven years' hard labor. In Australia, they worked for soldiers who had come to settle the land, which under English law was considered *terra nullius,* or "land belonging to nobody."

To the Europeans, the Aboriginals they came across seemed to be little more than savages. They had no buildings or cities, and ran around almost totally naked. Phillip, however, had been ordered to treat them in a friendly manner. He was instructed to "open an intercourse with the natives, and to conciliate their affections, enjoining all our subjects to live in amity and kindness with them."[6] Unfortunately, many of the others did not share his concern for the Aboriginals. They often treated them with cruelty, and occasionally killed them for being what they thought was an annoyance. This naturally led to bad feelings, and relations between the two cultures grew strained.

Poor relations with the Aboriginals was not the only problem that the settlers faced. As the weather got warmer, fresh water became scarce, and the wheat seed that had been planted failed to develop. Many of the sheep and cattle that had been brought along for food died or were killed by the natives. Supplies were quickly used up, and no replacements were available. With fresh vegetables in short supply, many of the settlers came down with scurvy. Medical supplies were also lacking, and prospects for the success of the settlement looked dim indeed.

It became obvious to Phillip that more free settlers were needed to help the colony grow. As he wrote to Undersecretary Sir Evan Nepean, "If fifty farmers were sent out with their families, they would do more in one year in rendering this colony independent of the mother country . . . than a thousand convicts."[7] Unfortunately, the situation worsened before it got better.

THE RUM CORPS

About two and a half years after the First Fleet landed at Sydney Harbour, the Second Fleet arrived. In addition to needed supplies, it also brought more than 700 new convicts to add to the struggling colony. (Eventually, a total of about 160,000

British soldiers inspect convicts transported to New South Wales during the eighteenth century.

convicts would be sent to Australia before the policy of transportation officially ended in 1868.) A regiment of soldiers known as the New South Wales Corps also made the journey. They came to replace the marines who had been the prisoners' keepers.

Some of the officers of the New South Wales Corps were corrupt and used their power for their own personal gain rather than for the good of the colony. A group headed by John Macarthur began to control trade in the settlement, where rum was the most valued commodity. The commanders of the corps provided many of the officers with grants of land and convicts to work them. This practice had not been allowed under Phillip, who had been forced to return to England in 1792 because of medical problems. Under the "Rum Corps," as these officers became known, alcoholism became a serious problem in the colony.

The New South Wales Corps remained in control until William Bligh became governor of the colony in 1806. When Bligh attempted to restrain the corps, he was put under house arrest and remained there for eighteen months. This so-called Rum Rebellion was too much for the mother country to ignore. A regiment headed by Colonel Lachlan Macquarie was sent from London to restore order in 1809, and the New South Wales Corps was disbanded.

"THE FATHER OF AUSTRALIA"

At the time Macquarie took over as governor of New South Wales, the convict population had grown so large that additional penal colonies had been established. The colony at Port Arthur in Tasmania housed the more vicious prisoners, as well as those who had committed further crimes after being transported. Another colony at Norfolk Island was used for the most malicious convicts of all. These prisoners were treated most cruelly by the soldiers and officers in charge. Conditions were so bad that prisoners would sometimes kill each other intentionally, in full view of their guards, so that they would be hanged and could escape their horrible surroundings.

Macquarie realized he had better utilize the prison population if the colony was to survive and prosper. He tried to use the convict workforce in a way that would be beneficial to all. He instituted a number of public works projects, using convict labor to build roads, schools, hospitals, and

ULURU

Near the geographical center of the continent, 288 miles southwest of Alice Springs, lies one of Australia's most recognizable symbols, Uluru. Named Ayers Rock by the Europeans, it is the largest rock in the world, over two miles long, one mile wide, and standing 1,148 feet above the desert floor. One of its attractions is the color change that occurs as the sun sets, making the rock a deeper and deeper red. Many tourists climb the rock, but the trek is not for the faint of heart. Over the years, numerous people have died either from falls or from heart attacks suffered during the ascent.

The Pitjandjara tribe of Aboriginals who live near the giant sandstone monolith would prefer that people not attempt the climb. To them, Uluru is a sacred place that played an important role in the Dreaming. Different points on the rock are associated with various legends and stories about the ancestors. The Aboriginals believe they are the direct descendants of the ancestors that formed the rock, and that it is their sacred responsibility to manage and care for the surrounding land.

Uluru, renamed Ayers Rock by the Europeans, is the world's largest monolith.

churches. Prisoners who possessed needed skills were always in demand.

By working off their sentences, convicts were able to obtain "tickets of leave" that gave them freedom within the colony. Some were even granted pardons that restored all their rights. A few of these ex-convicts—known as emancipists—attained great wealth after receiving their freedom.

Within time, Macquarie's efforts bore fruit. Many emancipists became farmers, shopkeepers, and laborers as businesses developed and commerce increased. Under Macquarie, the colony produced its own currency and rum was banned

The Port Arthur penitentiary in Tasmania housed prisoners during the nineteenth century. The guard tower is pictured here.

as money. In 1817, the Bank of New South Wales was established, signaling the beginning of Sydney's standing as the continent's financial center.

The end of the Napoleonic Wars in Europe in 1815 sparked a new wave of immigration. The free settlers—known as exclusives—helped bring the population of the colony up to thirty thousand by 1821. By this time, however, Macquarie's liberal attitude toward the emancipists had aroused the wrath of some powerful men in the British government, who looked down upon the emancipists regardless of their accomplishments. Macquarie eventually resigned from office under pressure and returned to England as thousands cheered him from the docks. They appreciated the work he had done and the reforms he had pushed through to help stabilize the economy and give the colony direction. Macquarie had brought order to the colony and had helped set the stage for its further growth and development. He was truly worthy of the title "the Father of Australia."

FEDERATION AND BEYOND

Slowly but surely, the colonies of Australia were making progress. More and more free settlers arrived from England to continue the work begun by the convicts. As new parts of the continent were opened up through the efforts of brave explorers, a sense of a national identity began to take hold. Gradually, the Europeans began to think of themselves as Australians rather than British. These feelings would eventually lead to self-government and the establishment of the Commonwealth of Australia as the twentieth century began. One hundred years later, the country has achieved status as a full-fledged member of the global community.

OPENING UP THE CONTINENT

As the first colony became more established and stable, some adventurous settlers began to strike out to explore the vast continent. Englishmen Matthew Flinders and George Bass had charted much of the coastline near Sydney and around Tasmania. In 1801, Flinders became the first person to sail around Australia. (He is also remembered as being the first to use the name Australia in referring to the continent. In his book, *A Voyage to Terra Australis,* he reflected, "Had I permitted myself any innovation upon the original name, it would have been to convert it into Australia; as being more agreeable to the ear.")[8]

It was not until 1813, however, that journeys were made into the interior. That year, George Blaxland, William Wentworth, and William Lawson became the first white men to travel across the Blue Mountains. Just over a decade later, Hamilton Hume and William Lovell made their way from New South Wales to Port Phillip, the site of present-day Melbourne.

Although much of the land opened up did not lend itself to farming, it proved to be ideal for raising sheep. By the

Early Australian settlers found the land to be ideal for sheep farming, and wool became a valuable export.

1820s, much of the region beyond the mountains was occupied by farmers. These men, known as squatters, claimed large tracts of land—sometimes as much as twenty thousand acres—for use by their livestock. The merino sheep that had been brought to Australia from Spain were a hardy breed that thrived in the dry climate and produced a fine wool that proved to be a valuable export.

NEW SETTLEMENTS

With the encouragement of the government, more and more free settlers spread out, and new colonies were established. The Swan River on Australia's west coast was explored by Captain James Stirling in 1827. His glowing report ("Of all that I have seen in various parts of the world, it possesses the greatest natural attraction.")[9] led to the eventual establishment of Western Australia and the city of Perth in 1829. Six years later, farmer John Batman acquired more than half a million acres of land from the Aborigines near the site of present-day Melbourne. A settlement was established there in 1837. South Australia, with its capital of Adelaide, was established that same year as the continent's first nonconvict colony. In 1851, New South Wales was divided into two parts. The southern portion was christened Victoria, while the northern portion retained the old name. Queensland, with its capital of Brisbane, separated from New South Wales eight years after that. In the far north, three attempts to establish settlements in what is now the Northern Territory met with failure because of clashes with Aboriginals, poor soil, and the great distances from the other settled areas.

No matter where the settlements were established, all the colonies were guilty of failing to recognize the rights of

TRUGANINI

Truganini was a Tasmanian Aboriginal, the daughter of an elder of a tribe in the Bruny Island region of the island. She was born during the height of the fighting between the Aboriginals and the white settlers that had begun when the settlers arrived in 1803. By the time Truganini was seventeen, several members of her immediate family had been murdered, and she herself had been raped.

Around 1830, the reverend George Robinson was given the job of rounding up the remaining Aboriginals and relocating them to Flinders Island. Truganini helped him, believing it was the only way her people could survive. Robinson ultimately abandoned the tribe, and in 1847, the forty-five Aboriginals that remained were moved to Oyster Cove on the Tasmanian mainland. Living conditions were poor and the natives died out, one by one. When Truganini's husband, Woorrady, died, he was thought to be the last male of the island people. His body was dissected by doctors, much to Truganini's chagrin. She asked that her body not be cut up when she died, but be buried instead. Truganini passed away in 1876, but her body was eventually removed from its grave and the skeleton displayed at the Tasmanian Museum. She became known, mistakenly, as the last full-blooded Tasmanian Aboriginal.

Truganini's skeleton was finally returned to the Aboriginal community nearly one hundred years after her death. It was cremated, and the ashes were scattered over her homeland. The Truganini Reserve near Hobart is named in her honor.

Aboriginals. Those who lived there were either killed or chased off the land they had occupied for centuries. Rather than just submit to the intrusion of the Europeans, the Aboriginals fought back. The result was a prolonged period of racial strife.

The Aboriginals faced further problems caused by the arrival of the Europeans. Thousands died of smallpox and other diseases that came to Australia along with the Europeans. Liquor also became a concern. With rum now readily available, countless Aboriginals had their lives ruined by alcoholism. The combination of disease, liquor, and a scarcity of food caused a significant decline in the Aboriginal population. It would be another century before it again approached pre-European levels.

EXPLORING THE INTERIOR

Although new colonies had been established near the Australian coastlines, few successful forays had been made into the continent's interior. Since westward-flowing rivers had been found on the western side of the Blue Mountains, speculation mounted that the interior might be home to a large inland sea. The search for this sea led to the discovery of the Murray and Darling Rivers—Australia's two largest rivers—by Charles Sturt between 1828 and 1830.

In 1859, the South Australian government became interested in building an overland telegraph from Adelaide, across the unexplored interior, to the northern coast. With this goal in mind, it offered a reward to the first person able to cross the continent from south to north. An epic attempt was made by police officer Robert O'Hara Burke and surveyor William Wills in 1860. They traveled from Melbourne as far north as the Flinders River before turning back. Unfortunately, they died of starvation before completing their trek. John McDouall Stuart would finally complete the south-north crossing two years later.

THE GOLD RUSH

Although the large Australian inland sea was never found, 1851 saw a discovery of another kind that would change the face of the nation. On February 12 of that year, thirty-five-year-old Edward Hargraves found gold just west of the Blue Mountains, near Bathurst in New South Wales. The news

THE AUSTRALIAN JESSE JAMES

Ned Kelly was a legend in his own short lifetime. He was representative of the bush and all that bush life symbolizes. (Although *outback* and *bush* are often used interchangeably, the outback generally refers to the arid and semiarid inland regions of the continent, while the bush can also refer to the forested areas in the east.) Today, however, more than 120 years after Kelly's death, the truth behind his legend remains shrouded in controversy.

Edward "Ned" Kelly was born in Beveridge, Victoria, in December 1854. When his father died, young Ned took on many odd jobs to provide for his family. The legality of some of these activities, such as corralling unbranded stray horses, was open to question. Kelly became a bushranger, as the outlaws of those days were called. He was first imprisoned by the local police at age seventeen.

Although all evidence suggests Kelly was nothing more than a thief and a killer, he portrayed himself as a Robin Hood of the outback. He and his gang began robbing banks and once destroyed a bank's records of outstanding loans so that they could not be repaid. His distrust of authority and loyalty to his friends were widely admired qualities and helped gain him many followers. Australians' fondness for the underdog helped make Kelly the country's foremost folk hero.

Kelly's brushes with the law occasionally led to bloodshed, and he is known to have murdered three policemen. After avoiding capture for more than a year, he was eventually apprehended in Glenrowan. On November 11, 1880, Ned Kelly was hanged inside the Old Melbourne Gaol (jail).

Bushranger and folk hero Ned Kelly wore this makeshift suit of armor during his years evading British authorities.

spread like wildfire, and within days the countryside was crawling with prospectors looking to strike it rich. (Gold had actually been found earlier, but the authorities suppressed news of the finds because they feared lawlessness such as that which marked the California gold rush.) By the end of the year, even larger deposits were found in Victoria. The gold deposits in Australia were even larger than the ones in California. The famous Holtermann nugget, found at Hill End in 1872, is the largest single mass of gold ever discovered in the world, weighing in at more than two hundred pounds.

In 1854, the rush for gold led to an incident that is remembered as the Eureka Rebellion. Passions were high among prospectors at the Ballarat goldfields. Living conditions were poor, and the administration in charge was corrupt. Prospectors particularly resented a high license fee that authorities required to dig for the precious metal. In December, a band of Irish miners finally revolted against the administration. They publicly burned their licenses, then assembled in their crudely constructed wooden Eureka stockade. There, the rebels were met by government

EDMUND KENNEDY AND JACKEY JACKEY

The center of the Australian continent received much attention from explorers in the mid-1800s, but there was also much uncharted territory in the northeastern region of Queensland. One of the men who ventured into this part of the unknown was Edmund Kennedy. In 1848, he led a six-hundred-mile expedition from Rockingham Bay to Cape York. The going was tough as Kennedy—together with twelve other men including an Aboriginal guide named Jackey Jackey—encountered thick jungles, high mountains, crocodile-infested waters, and hostile natives. After two months, they had progressed only twenty miles into the interior. At that point, part of the expedition stayed behind while Kennedy and four others continued north to meet a supply ship.

At Shelburne Bay, three of the men (including one who had accidentally shot himself) could go no farther. Kennedy and Jackey Jackey took on the final leg to Cape York by themselves. Now that the party was much smaller, a group of Aboriginals who had been following them decided to attack. Kennedy was mortally wounded by a spear. Jackey Jackey removed the weapon and cared for him, but Kennedy soon died. Though wounded himself, the guide continued on to Albany Bay, where he was met by a rescue ship.

Jackey Jackey led the crew of the ship back to where he had buried Kennedy. The grave, however, was empty and Kennedy's body was never found. Jackey Jackey was eventually honored for his bravery and loyalty.

troops. The battle lasted just fifteen minutes. The stockade was destroyed, and twenty-eight men lost their lives. Despite this defeat, the miners were eventually victorious as license fees were reduced and conditions improved. Many consider the Eureka Rebellion to be the birthplace of Australian democracy.

Until the gold rush time, labor had been in short supply on the continent. The possibility of finding gold, however, attracted people from all over the world. Many of those who came to seek their fortune were Chinese. Miners and colonists alike started to resent the Oriental presence in Australia, deeming it a threat to their jobs and culture. Race riots followed, and eventually a white Australia policy was instituted that limited immigration to Europeans.

In addition to prospectors, many others came to take advantage of the increased business opportunities that arose. This led to the construction of railroads, hospitals, roads, schools, and bridges. At the time of the first strike, Australia's population was approximately half a million. Inside of ten years, that number had tripled. With the workforce growing by the day, there was no longer a need for convicts to work for the large landholders. By 1868, the practice of transportation ended in Australia. In the eighty years it was in effect, approximately 160,000 prisoners had made the trip from England.

FORMING A NATION

Over the years, it had become more and more difficult for England to administer the Australian colonies because of their great distance from the motherland. In 1855, Parliament passed legislation that gave them the power to govern themselves while still being under British authority. (Among other things, Britain continued to appoint the governor and to exercise control over external relations. It could also disallow any colonial law that it felt threatened imperial interests.) New South Wales, Victoria, Tasmania, and South Australia did so by 1859. Queensland followed in 1859 after its separation from New South Wales. The last state to adopt self-government—Western Australia—did so in 1890. For some people, however, self-government was not enough.

The idea of unifying the colonies into one federation was discussed as early as 1847. Because of the intense competition between colonies, however, the concept never received serious consideration. Each region had its own needs and desires, and was concerned with its own interests. A strong sense of nationalism was not a driving factor for unification as it was in other British colonies such as the thirteen American colonies. Instead, the forces that eventually brought Australia together included the desire for a uniform immigration policy, the appeal of a single economic and political system, and the need for a single, unified Australian voice in foreign affairs.

Great Britain did little to discourage talk of federation. Realizing the difficulty in maintaining control in a land so distant, the British government encouraged the colonies to consolidate into more effective provinces that could govern their internal affairs. After holding conventions to consider federation in 1891 and 1897, the colonies drew up a constitution. The Commonwealth of Australia Constitution Act was passed by the British Parliament and agreed to by Queen Victoria in September 1900.

The Commonwealth of Australia came into existence on January 1, 1901, the first day of the twentieth century. Edmund Barton was named the country's first prime minister. The British monarch was the official head of state, but without direct authority over Australian laws. His or her representative in Australia held the title of governor-general. The state governors were also technically representatives of the British monarch. They were recommended by Australian officials and ratified by the British king or queen.

That September, the first Australian flag flew over the Exhibition Building in Melbourne, the temporary capital of the nation. The blue flag features a star with six (now seven) points, one for each state and another representing the territories, on the lower left. The right side features the five stars of the Southern Cross, a constellation visible from Australia. The new nation still retained strong ties with Great Britain, as denoted by the British Union Jack in the flag's upper left-hand corner. (The nation's national anthem would remain "God Save the Queen" until 1984.) Britain continued to handle Australia's foreign affairs, and the motherland expected Australians to provide it with military support.

AUSTRALIA AT WAR

Australian military forces fought alongside British soldiers during the Boer War at the turn of the century. When World

War I broke out a decade later, the Australian and New Zealand Army Corps (ANZAC) fought bravely along with the Allies. As Australia's prime minister declared, "Our duty is quite clear—to gird up our loins and remember that we are Britons."[10] Approximately 330,000 Australians fought in the war, and 60,000 were killed in battle, many by Turkish troops in the infamous battle at Gallipoli. The battle is memorialized in a large display in the War Memorial in Canberra.

Despite the tragic losses of life, the war had several positive effects on Australia. The bravery and achievements of the ANZAC troops helped the young nation develop a sense of national identity that had previously been lacking. Australia also grew economically as industries involved in the manufacture of wartime goods showed a surge in production. Thousands of immigrants entered the country, bringing the population to the 6 million mark by 1925. The economic spurt continued through the 1920s until it was brought to a sudden halt by the Great Depression. Nearly one out of every three people lost their jobs. Swagmen (workers who carried

Australian soldiers board a ship in Melbourne to join the Allies during World War I.

all their possessions in bags on their backs) became a common sight as people left the cities in search of work in the country. By 1933, wool prices had begun to rise, and the industry showed signs of recovering.

This positive trend continued until it was interrupted by World War II. Again, Australian troops enlisted to fight on the side of the motherland. When Japan entered the war, however, it changed matters completely. The country's proximity to Australia now presented a distinct threat to the national security. In 1942, the war touched Australian soil for the first time. The Japanese bombed the cities of Darwin, Broome, and Townsville in the northern part of the continent, killing more than 250 people. Japanese submarines made their way into Sydney Harbour.

The situation produced a major shift in Australian foreign policy. Rather than send more men to Europe to fight with the British, Australian troops stayed in the Pacific, where they fought side by side with the Americans who had been sent to help defend the country. One of their major victories was at the Battle of the Coral Sea.

IMMIGRATION AND ECONOMIC GROWTH

By the time World War II ended, nearly thirty-five thousand more Australians had lost their lives in the fighting. The nation realized its future defense would rely, to a large degree, on a strong economy and a larger population. Immigration was encouraged, and thousands of refugees from war-torn European nations were admitted into the country for humanitarian reasons. The government offered incentives to those who wanted to settle in Australia, such as free land, free passage for former service people, and reduced rates for others. This flood of immigrants changed the nation's entire social structure, which previously had been mostly British.

Because of the annihilation of the Jews by the Nazis during the war, racism had become a sensitive issue around the world. Australia responded by gradually easing its white Australia policy. (It would be formally abolished in 1973 when the last official barriers against immigration by race were removed.) In the quarter century following the end of the war, nearly 3 million people came to settle in the Land Down Under. Today, approximately one-quarter of Australia's population is composed of immigrants and their children.

Just as in the period following World War I, the years after World War II saw a surge in the economy. Australia enjoyed a period of peace and prosperity under Robert Menzies, who was elected prime minister in 1949 and remained in office until 1966. The discovery of new mineral resources boosted industry, as did the opening of new markets for Australian goods in nearby Asian nations. The government's stability also attracted more British and American investments in the country, further strengthening the economy.

Relations with the United States were bolstered when Australia quickly came to America's aid in the Korean War. America showed its gratitude with the signing of the Australia–New Zealand–United States (ANZUS) defense treaty in 1951. Three years later, Australia joined with the United States, Great Britain, France, New Zealand, Pakistan, the Philippines, and Thailand to form the Southeast Asia Treaty Organization (SEATO), aimed mainly at preventing the spread of communism in the Pacific. Australia showed its support for the alliance when it committed troops to the Vietnam War in 1965. But as the war dragged on, opposition to it began to increase. Many Australians pro-tested the draft, which was instituted in 1964. Conscription (forced military enrollment) would eventually be abolished eight years later.

Robert Menzies served as Australia's prime minister for seventeen peaceful and prosperous years.

ASSIMILATION AND ABORIGINAL RIGHTS

Protests against the war were a sign of the climate of social consciousness that was beginning to take hold. Movements for women's liberation and gay rights forced the government to reexamine its past policies. A move to end racial discrimination became a primary concern as more people became aware of injustices suffered by the Aboriginals over the years.

The government had made a program of assimilation an objective as far back as 1951. As the Commonwealth minister

Australian Aboriginals obtained the right to vote in 1962 and adopted their own flag ten years later.

for territories explained, "Assimilation means, in practical terms, that, in the course of time, it is expected that all persons of Aboriginal blood or mixed blood in Australia will live like White Australians do."[11] In practice, however, assimilation meant an even greater loss of rights. The government forced many Aboriginals to leave their homes and move to townships, where they were initiated into European culture. In this way, it was reasoned, their economic situation would be improved. This forced assimilation proved to be a complete failure.

Inspired, in part, by the struggle for rights undertaken by Native Americans in the United States, Aboriginals began to make themselves heard. They clamored for recognition and finally, by 1962, obtained the right to vote. Five years later, they were given the status of citizens, and in 1972 they adopted their own flag. (The top half of the flag is black and the bottom half red, representing the dark-skinned natives and the color of the earth, respectively. In the center is a yellow circle that stands for the Sun.) The Department of Aboriginal Affairs was set up to help attend to the needs of Aboriginal peoples. Their struggle for equality, however, still has far to go.

ECONOMY AND POLITICS

The period from 1949 to 1972 was one of political stability for Australia. The country was governed by a coalition of the Liberal and National Country parties that guided it through more than two decades of prosperity. In the years that followed, however, the country was shocked by an extraordinary action on the part of the British government.

In the early 1970s, the demand for Australian ores and minerals declined, and labor strikes added to the nation's economic problems. Social protests against Australian involvement in Vietnam and discrimination against Aboriginals added to the climate of unrest. In an attempt to solve some of the country's problems, the government of Prime Minister E. Gough Whitlam tried to institute a series of reforms. Many members of Parliament, however, believed the programs were too expensive. With Parliament and the prime minister unable to agree on the steps that needed to be taken, the Australian governor-general, John Kerr, took an unprecedented and unexpected action. As the representative of the British monarch, Kerr dismissed Whitlam as prime minister and installed J. Malcolm Fraser of the opposition party in his place. In effect, a representative of a foreign nation (Great Britain) was interfering in the Australian political process. Many Australians were shocked by this move, which they considered an inappropriate use of a power that no longer applied in the modern age. Nevertheless, the caretaker government won the next election and remained in power.

INTO THE TWENTY-FIRST CENTURY

In recent years, Australia has become more involved in international affairs, particularly those in Asia and the South Pacific. Trade with the Pacific Rim countries has increased and has helped Australia attain its status as a country with one of the highest standards of living in the world.

Australia continued to shed most of its time-honored ties with England. In 1986, Queen Elizabeth signed a proclamation terminating several of Australia's legal and political connections with the motherland. Six years later, the nation's oath of allegiance was modified, leaving out reference to the queen. As the twenty-first century begins, an increasing number of citizens want the country to become entirely independent of Britain, with an Australian as the head of state. Whether or not this occurs, the country still looks optimistically toward the future, confident of its ability to solve its problems and to continue to improve its position on the world stage.

THE AUSTRALIAN
WAY OF LIFE

Contrary to popular belief, the great majority of Australia's 19 million inhabitants do not live in the outback, but rather in the nation's large cities, within an hour or two of the ocean. The vast interior, with its scorching temperatures and arid climate, is home to only the hardiest 4 percent of the population. No matter where they live, they all must earn a living, feed their families, provide their children with an education, and so on. They do so, however, while still taking the time to enjoy life and the richness and beauty of their island continent. This is reflected in the informal, friendly atmosphere, where "G'day, mate!" is the greeting most often heard, and "No worries" is the prevailing philosophy.

LIFE IN THE OUTBACK

Life in the outback is not for the timid. There is little water and meager vegetation, and the dangerous animals and insects pose an ever-present threat to life and limb. This lifestyle appeals to a certain type of person—a person who is independent, opinionated, and often distrustful of authority. These characteristics date back to the early days of the country's settlement. The ex-convicts who had been transported there from England learned to appreciate the open spaces after having been locked up for long periods of time. The heroes of the day were those explorers who pushed into the interior and dared to go where none had gone before.

In many ways, life in the outback has not changed much since those early days. The towns that exist are very small, while ranches tend to be extremely large. Because of the vast distances between towns, people often have to provide their own entertainment. Fishing and hunting are popular, as is horseback riding. Trips into town are a big occasion, giving ranchers and miners a chance to catch up with friends and relatives.

Friendship and loyalty are valued qualities in the outback. Although the people are independent, they realize they must also rely heavily on one another, particularly in times of emergency. Homesteads are linked by two-way radio so that families can share information in case of accidents or illness. An accident in the desert can easily be fatal if help does not arrive in time.

Life in the outback is difficult and not for everyone. The great majority of Australians prefer city life and the pleasures and challenges that go with it.

SYDNEY

Since its settlement by convicts and soldiers of the First Fleet in 1788, the town of Sydney—named after the British home secretary, Thomas Townshend, first viscount Sydney

COOBER PEDY

One of the strangest towns in Australia—if not the entire world—is Coober Pedy, located a little more than five hundred miles northwest of Adelaide in the harsh outback of South Australia. The town is the opal capital of Australia. Approximately 70 percent of the world's supply originates there.

The first opal was discovered in the area by fifteen-year-old Willie Hutchinson in 1915. His discovery led to many settlements, which eventually gave rise to the town. Soldiers returning from World War I introduced the idea of living in underground dugouts, similar to the trenches in France, to cope with the dust storms and harsh weather conditions. Temperatures can reach as high as 122 degrees Fahrenheit in the daytime and as low as 32 degrees Fahrenheit at night. These dugouts, together with the numerous mines, gave the town its name, which is an Anglicized version of the Aboriginal "kupa piti," which translates to "white man hole in the ground."

The underground living areas are the most striking feature of Coober Pedy. About half of the town's population of approximately two thousand live in these troglodyte homes. There are also two underground churches and subterranean shops, restaurants, and hotels. Because of the underground buildings and hundreds of abandoned mines, the region has an eerie, desolate appearance. This "end-of-the-world" look has been captured in movies such as *Mad Max Beyond Thunderdome*, much of which was filmed in the area.

(a viscount is a member of the peerage, below earl but above baron)—has made gigantic strides. By the time transportation to the colony ended in 1840, the city had grown in size to approximately thirty thousand people and had begun to establish a reputation as a center of trade in the region. The gold rush of 1851 brought still more settlers seeking their fortune.

Today, Sydney is the capital of New South Wales and is the largest city in Australia, with a population of almost 4 million. Nearly one-third of the workforce is involved in manufacturing, and oil refining is one of the most important industries. The city is also a center for learning. The University of Sydney, the University of New South Wales, and Macquarie University are three of the nation's leading educational institutions.

Sydneysiders are proud of their metropolis, which is built on low hills surrounding one of the largest, most magnificent harbors in the world. The Harbour Bridge and the Opera

The Opera House, with its distinctive white arched roof, can be seen in this view of Sydney's grand harbor.

House, with its white shell-shaped roofs, are the two most recognizable manufactured structures on the continent, and two of the most popular attractions for sightseers. Nearby Bondi Beach, with its glistening surf and sparkling white sand, is a mecca for the sun and surf crowd.

MELBOURNE

Located on Port Phillip Bay at the mouth of the Yarra River, Melbourne (population 3.3 million) is the capital of the state of Victoria. It was settled as Port Phillip in 1835 and adopted its present name, after England's prime minister William Lamb, the second viscount Melbourne, in 1837. When gold was discovered in Victoria in the 1850s, Melbourne was on its way to becoming a center of trade. By the end of the nineteenth century, "Marvellous Melbourne" ranked second only to Sydney among Australian cities in terms of size and importance. When the Commonwealth was formed in 1901, the city was selected as the new nation's temporary capital, until it was replaced by Canberra in 1913.

Modern Melbourne is a more serious city than Sydney, with a lifestyle that is not quite as relaxed. It has more of an air of reserve, with greater respect for tradition. As Sydneysiders are fond of saying, "Sydney is made of plastic, while Melbourne is made of stone."[12] It is a business and financial center, and the manufacture of cars, electronic equipment, machinery, and textiles are among its most important industries. Broken Hill Proprietary Company, Ltd. (BHP), a steel manufacturing and mining giant and the largest company in Australia, has its headquarters in the city. In the field of education, the University of Melbourne, La Trobe University, the Royal Melbourne Institute of Technology, and Monash University are among the nation's finest institutions of higher learning. Melbourne is also popular with the sporting crowd. The Australian Open is held each year at the National Tennis Centre. Flemington Racecourse is the site of the Melbourne Cup, Australia's famous horse race. In 1956, Melbourne became the first city in the Southern Hemisphere to host the Summer Olympic Games.

BRISBANE

The city of Brisbane, named after the former governor of New South Wales, Sir Thomas Brisbane, was once the site of

Once a penal colony, Brisbane is now a thriving cosmopolitan city.

a penal colony. The colony's commandant, Captain Patrick Logan, earned a reputation for cruelty that was immortalized in the ballad "Moreton Bay." The city was eventually opened to free settlers and was named the capital of the newly established colony of Queensland in 1859.

Today, Brisbane is the third largest city in Australia with a population of nearly 1.6 million. Until relatively recently, it was thought of as a kind of overblown country town. Now, it is a lively, cosmopolitan city that doesn't take itself as seriously as the southern capitals. It is located in one of the most productive agricultural and mining regions of the entire continent. Produce is transported to the city over a network of railway lines and highways, and then exported by oceangoing vessels that have access to the port.

Brisbane's development was sparked by a mining boom in the 1960s. In addition, thousands of tourists poured into the city when it hosted the Commonwealth Games in 1982 and a world's fair in 1988. Reminders of the city's early days still remain, however. A favorite site for pictures is the Old Windmill, which was built by convict labor in 1828.

PERTH

Australia's fourth-largest city (population 1.1 million), Perth has been called the most isolated city in the world. It lies 1,674 miles away from Adelaide, the nearest urban center. Perth was founded in 1829 as the Swan River Settlement in southwestern Australia. In part because it was situated so far from any other settlement, labor was scarce and communications poor. Convict labor helped improve the conditions, and the city's growth was spurred by the discovery of gold in Kalgoorlie in 1890. The completion of the transcontinental railway in 1917 helped link Perth to the rest of the nation.

Named after a county in Scotland, Perth has become one of Australia's centers of heavy industry. Everything from steel to petroleum to rubber goods is manufactured in this capital of Western Australia. Items are exported through the port

High-rise offices dominate the skyline of Perth, Australia's fourth-largest city.

facilities in the suburb of Fremantle. The city is home to the University of Western Australia and Murdoch University. Its cultural attractions include the Art Gallery of Western Australia, the Western Australian Museum, and a modern concert hall that houses the Perth City Ballet.

CANBERRA

A lake divides Australia's capital, Canberra, with the government buildings on the south side and the city's business center to the north.

When the Commonwealth of Australia was formed in 1901, it was decided that the nation's capital would be established in the state of New South Wales. Archrivals Sydney and Melbourne both wanted the honor, so to avoid problems, the Australian Capital Territory (ACT) was established between the two cities. A competition was held to design the capital city, which was to be called Canberra from an Aboriginal word believed to mean "meeting place." American architect

Walter Burley Griffin won first prize for his design of the nine-hundred-square-mile area whose population today has grown to over three hundred thousand. A lake named in his honor cuts the city in half. On the south side of the lake are the main government buildings. The city's business center lies north of the lake. In addition to the buildings of the federal government, the city is also home to the National Library of Australia, the Australian National Gallery, the Australian National University, Mount Stromlo Observatory, and the Australian National War Memorial.

GOVERNMENT

Unlike other Australian cities, Canberra would not have come into existence were it not for the establishment of the nation as a commonwealth. As a federation of six states and two territories, it is governed by a constitution that was approved in 1901. The government is a parliamentary system based on that of Great Britain, but the system of federal, state, and local governments resembles that of the United States.

The federal government is run by the prime minister, who is the leader of the party with the most members in Parliament. The cabinet, which consists of parliamentary members whom the prime minister selects, is the nation's major policy-making body.

Parliament, the center of legislative power, is divided into an upper house (the Senate) and a lower house (the House of Representatives). The Senate consists of 12 delegates from each of the six states and 2 from each of the two territories, for a total of 76. They serve six-year and three-year terms, respectively. The lower house is composed of 148 members who are elected to three-year terms of office.

The six individual states, each of which has a governor, have their own legislative and judicial systems. All the states except Queensland have two-chamber legislatures consisting of a legislative council (the upper house) and either a legislative assembly or a house of assembly (the lower house). Queensland and the Northern Territory each have one-chamber legislatures.

The federal government handles matters concerning defense, foreign relations, and national economic policy. The state governments have supervision over education, police, and social welfare. Very little power is in the hands of the local governments.

Most are responsible for matters involving building codes, town planning, traffic regulations, and similar functions.

The judicial branch of the government comprises circuit courts, magistrates' courts, county courts, children's courts, and higher state courts. The highest court of the land—and the official interpreter of the constitution—is the High Court, which resembles the American Supreme Court. The High Court consists of a chief justice and six fellow justices, each of whom is appointed by the governor-general in council.

HEALTH CARE AND SOCIAL SERVICES

Australia was one of the first countries to establish social service plans to take care of those unable to do so for themselves. Pensions for the elderly were first provided in 1909. The next year, provisions were made for those too sick to work. Today, aid is also provided to single parents, low-income families, and the unemployed.

Australia's health care system has helped the nation attain a life expectancy of eighty-three years of age for women and seventy-six years for men. Private doctors provide most health care, while Medicare—the national health insurance program—covers approximately 85 percent of the expenses. There are more than one thousand hospitals, with more than seventy-five thousand beds, located throughout the country.

The most common cause of death is atherosclerosis, a disease in which fatty deposits choke the individual's arteries. Alcohol abuse is a problem of great concern, as Australia has one of the highest beer consumption rates in the entire world. Illegal drugs are another problem, with heroin one of the most widely used. The opium poppy, from which it is derived, is produced in nearby Southeast Asia.

A special problem regarding health care is posed by the nation's size and the remoteness of many of its small towns. The Royal Flying Doctor Service was established in 1927 to provide health care for those living in these isolated regions. Bases around the country use two-way radio linkups to send a fleet of some forty medical aircraft to areas of the outback where basic medical services would otherwise be unavailable.

EDUCATION

The importance of education in Australia can be traced back to the colony's early days. There was great concern about the morality of the children of convicts, who roamed unattended while their parents worked. Churches were the places where these children could best be given a strict, moral, religious education. Until the time of the gold rush, the Australian colonial governments subsidized schools run by the major religious denominations. Funding was later given to schools based on the principle of a "free, compulsory, and secular" education. It was free to make it available to even the poorest citizens, compulsory so that parents could not deny their children the right to an education, and secular to avoid conflicts with religious teachings. The system was successful and by 1900, Australia was one of the few nations to have a literacy rate of above 90 percent.

Today, about three-fourths of Australia's 3 million children make use of the nation's free public education system. The remaining students attend private schools supported by Protestant or Roman Catholic churches. Attendance is compulsory for those between the ages of six and fifteen (sixteen in Tasmania), but many children attend preschool at an even earlier age. Youngsters attend elementary school for either six or seven years (depending on the state). They then begin

A group of fourth graders enjoy lunch outside of their school in downtown Melbourne.

lower (or junior) secondary school at the seventh or eighth year and continue through the tenth year when they may leave with a School Leaving Certificate. Many students continue on for two more years at the upper (or senior) secondary level before continuing on to university study. Virtually everyone in Australia completes ten years of study, with more than 70 percent finishing all twelve years.

Elementary school children living in the outback are faced with a special problem. Since they often reside hundreds of miles from the nearest school, regular attendance is impractical if not impossible. For these youngsters, the government created the Schools of the Air. Under this program, lessons and homework are sent through the mail, and students participate in classroom instruction with teachers via two-way radios, televisions, video and cassette recorders, and computers. Once a month or so, the outback children are driven to town to spend a day with others in a regular classroom. The idea for the program was proposed by schoolteacher Adelaide Miethke in 1944. The School of the Air program officially opened seven years later. Today, there are twenty-six Schools of the Air with approximately two thousand students.

RELIGION

The religious beliefs of Australia's Aboriginals have been maintained down through the centuries. Although there have been converts to Catholicism and other religions among those who have been assimilated into the modern Australian culture, many still accept the beliefs of their ancestors. To those, the legacy of the Dreaming guides their daily life.

Until this century, most white Australians were members of the Church of England, or Anglican Church. Early Irish immigrants brought Roman Catholicism along with them to the colony, and today, Catholics outnumber Anglicans by a steadily increasing margin. Each group now claims more than a quarter of the nation's population as its members.

Since the end of World War II, the range of religious groups has expanded. Jewish, Greek Orthodox, Islamic, and Buddhist communities have increased in size as a result of increased immigration from Southeast Asia and the Middle East. Islam is arguably the fastest growing religion on the continent.

AUSTRALIA'S FIRST SAINT?

Mary MacKillop was born in Melbourne in 1842. She grew up in a poor family, and decided when she was fifteen that she would become a nun and devote her life to the needy. In 1861, she moved to Penola in South Australia. There she met—and became good friends with—a Catholic priest named Father Julian Woods. Together, the two opened the first free Catholic school in Australia.

Mary was an excellent teacher, but still felt a religious calling. Unable to find an order that suited her, she and Father Woods started their own, which they called the Sisters of Saint Joseph of the Sacred Heart (Australia's first religious order). She eventually had seventeen schools under her supervision. Unfortunately, her independence bothered the bishop in Adelaide, who had her excommunicated (cut off in membership from the Church) when she refused to turn over control of her schools. The bishop eventually apologized, and Mary was accepted back the following year.

By the time of Mary's death in 1909, there were St. Joseph's schools all through the country. Her followers began a campaign to have her canonized. In 1995, Pope John Paul II visited Australia for her beatification, the first step taken toward becoming a saint.

Perhaps surprisingly, however, as the number of religions has increased, the number of Australians who attend religious services has been on the decline. Of those who responded in the 1996 census, 25 percent stated their religious preference as "no religion." This position is likely related to the new, rebellious attitudes prevalent among the younger generation.

HOLIDAYS AND FESTIVALS

Like Americans, Australians celebrate Christmas, Easter, and New Year's Day. In addition, Australia Day (January 26) and ANZAC Day (April 25) are also national holidays. Australia Day commemorates the landing of Captain Phillip and the First Fleet in 1788, while ANZAC Day marks the landing of the Allied forces at Gallipoli in World War I, a battle in which thousands of Australian soldiers lost their lives.

In addition to these days, numerous festivals and holidays are celebrated at various times of the year in the different states and territories. In New South Wales, Tamworth hosts the Country Music Festival in the last two weeks of January. Australia's main country festival, it concludes with the presentation of the Golden Guitar Awards. In the Melbourne Moomba Festival (Victoria), breathtaking shows, street parties, and garden parties provide entertainment for people of all ages during the second week of March. In June, a celebration of Aboriginal heritage can be experienced every other year at the Laura Aboriginal Dance Festival in Cape York, Queensland. Every May, Little Cornwall is the site of Kernewek Lowender, the world's largest Cornish Festival. It celebrates the contributions made to the state's prosperity by the early copper miners. The last weekend of August is when the Shinju Matsuri (Festival of the Pearl) is held in Broome, Western Australia. The festival encourages a community spirit and keeps alive the romance of the pearling industry, which had been centered in the region. One of the country's most unusual festivals is the Henley-on-Todd Regatta at Alice Springs in the Northern Territory. The races on the bone-dry Todd River consist of team members running up and down the riverbed carrying a cardboard cutout of a boat with sails and masts. Even the ACT gets into the festival spirit with the Floriade in Canberra. This magnificent flower festival takes place in Commonwealth Park every October.

FOOD

Most people's conception of Australian food is limited to barbie (barbecue) fare such as shrimp, hamburgers, and snorkers (sausages). Knowledgeable gourmets, however, know the nation's cuisine has become much more sophisticated over the past three decades. This is due, in large measure, to the wave of immigrants who came from Italy, Greece, and other European nations, and brought their native dishes along with them. The influx of newcomers from Asia has been particularly influential in recent years. Dishes using ingredients such as lemongrass, ginger, and coconut milk are becoming more common.

Australian cuisine includes exotic meats such as kangaroo (a low-cholesterol alternative to beef), emu, and crocodile.

VEGEMITE

To Australians, Vegemite is as much a part of their country's heritage as kangaroos, boomerangs, and Ayers Rock. The bread spread was developed by Dr. Cyril Callister, a thirty-year-old chemist who worked for the Fred Walker Cheese Company. His 1922 invention, a blend of brewer's yeast, celery, onions, salt, and other ingredients, was a foul-smelling black paste, but had an appealing taste. It was also an excellent source of vitamin B. The following year, a contest was held to find a name for the new concoction, and Vegemite was selected.

Sales were sluggish at first, but gradually improved over the years. They were given a boost in 1939 when Vegemite received an official product endorsement from the British Medical Association as a nutritionally balanced food rich in vitamin B. During World War II, Australian servicemen had Vegemite included in their rations, cementing the product's popularity.

In the mid-1950s, the now-familiar "Happy Little Vegemites" jingle was heard for the first time, etching the product into the Australian consciousness. The nutritious spread achieved trivia immortality in 1984 when it became the first product to be electronically scanned at a grocery checkout.

Vegetables and fruits, such as warrigal and quandong, are also used in native dishes. Seafood is very popular, with yabbies and red emperor among the local specialties. Mass-market favorites include meat pies and Vegemite.

Along with the improving cuisine, Australia has a wine industry that is rapidly gaining international recognition. The warm climate is conducive to growing grapes, and each region has its own specialty. The whites of Hunter Valley in New South Wales, the reds of the Coonawarra district of South Australia, and the ports of the Rutherglen region of Victoria are just three of the most popular varieties.

For most Australians, however, beer is the national drink and Fosters the best-known brand. Many small breweries have sprung up to compete with the larger companies. Low-alcohol varieties have also become more popular in recent years.

Yabbies, a type of crayfish, are a popular Australian dish.

One of the favorite events in the life of the average Aussie is the barbecue. Family and friends gather together to grill shrimp and snorkers on the barbie. They raise their stubbies and tinnies (bottles and cans of beer) in celebration of the good life they have come to appreciate in the land known as Oz.

AUSTRALIAN CULTURE: A MIXTURE OF OLD AND NEW

Australian culture is an intermingling of two very different traditions: the ancient, oral culture of the Aboriginals who were the country's first inhabitants, and the heritage of the English settlers who colonized the country barely two hundred years ago. Both traditions reflect a love of the natural wonders of the vast, empty land, isolated in its own corner of the world. The English legacy has added a sense of individualism and independence displayed, out of necessity, by those who settled the first colonies. These traditions are expressed through the arts, recreation, and entertainment of a rich and vibrant cultural scene.

ART

For thousands of years before the arrival of the Europeans, Aboriginals decorated rocks and caves with their paintings and drawings. Sometimes items used in rituals such as shields and posts were decorated. Aboriginal art focused on the events of the natives' daily lives and their religious beliefs. Many of these works exist today, although a number have been painted over to preserve their images. One of the major Aboriginal art sites is in Arnhem Land near Darwin.

Many Aboriginal paintings are examples of what is called "X-ray art." These drawings show the skeletons and internal organs of the people and animals they represent. Others, found in eastern Queensland, show sticklike figures called quinkans. Quinkans are spirits thought to emerge from the ground.

Although the most common form of early Aboriginal painting was rock art, bark painting, which has become very popular of late, is probably the best known. This variation

was native to Arnhem Land and other regions where suitable bark from the stringy-bark (*Eucalyptus tetradonta*) tree could be found. It has become popular for tourists to buy examples of bark painting as souvenirs of their visit to Australia.

The first notable Aboriginal artist was Albert Namatjira, whose work brought him into the public eye in the 1930s and 1940s. His glorious watercolors portrayed the beauty of life in the outback. With the income he earned from his work, he helped support many of his people, as was his obligation under the laws of his tribe. In 1957, Namatjira became the first Aboriginal to be granted Australian citizenship.

The first Europeans to paint pictures of Australia came to the continent with Captain James Cook on the *Endeavour* in 1768. It was not until almost one hundred years later, however, that Australian painters began to receive recognition. Of the early artists, Conrad Martens was the best known. He is considered by some to be one of the founders of the Australian school of painting, specializing in washes and watercolors.

Shortly before the beginning of the twentieth century, the Heidelberg School (named after a suburb of Melbourne) came into existence. Its members—Charles Conder, Frederick McCubbin, Sir Arthur Streeton, and Tom Roberts—gained fame for their paintings of Australian frontier life in the style of the French impressionists. As Roberts explained, "Paint what you like and love what you paint . . . being in the bush and feeling the delight and fascination of the great pastoral life and work I have tried to express it."[13]

Among the best-known artists of the twentieth century, Sir Sidney Nolan stands out for his scenes from Australian folklore. His works include his Ned Kelly series, and his paintings of the Burke and Wills expedition and the battle at Gallipoli. His landscapes helped him build a reputation far beyond the country's borders. George Russell Drysdale is considered perhaps the greatest painter of the Australian outback, while Sir William Dobell won the Archibald Prize for portraiture. One of the most commercially successful artists of the modern day is Ken Done, whose brightly colored designs grace everything from T-shirts to pillowcases.

Many Australian cities have built excellent art museums. The National Gallery of Australia in Canberra houses what is arguably the most important collection of Australian art. It includes more than one hundred thousand works that reflect the spirit of the country and its people.

ARCHITECTURE

Since the arrival of the Europeans in the late eighteenth century, Australian architecture has been influenced by three key factors: climate, terrain, and the availability of building materials. The very first buildings were primitive affairs, constructed of mud, bark, sticks, and whatever other materials the settlers could gather. Some prefabricated structures were shipped from England, but they were few and far between.

THE SYDNEY OPERA HOUSE

The Sydney Opera House (a misnomer, since it is actually a complex of theaters and halls) is like no other building in the world. It was designed by Danish architect Jorn Utzon who, according to legend, came up with the idea for the arched roofs while peeling an orange. Construction began in 1959, but the building was not completed until fourteen years later because of a series of delays, including Utzon's resignation from the project. The building cost $102 million, the bulk of which was raised through an opera house lottery.

The Sydney Opera House consists of nearly 1,000 rooms, and covers 4.5 acres. It weighs 161,000 tons, and contains 67,000 square feet of glass and 400 miles of electrical cable. Included among its main attractions are a 2,679-seat Concert Hall, a 1,547-seat Opera Theatre, a 544-seat Drama Theatre, a 398-seat Playhouse, and several restaurants.

The first performance in the complex was the Australian Opera's production of *War and Peace* by Sergei Prokofiev on September 28, 1973. Operating twenty-four hours a day, every day of the year except Christmas and Good Friday, the Sydney Opera House currently averages about three thousand events a year, including musicals, operas, ballets, exhibitions, concerts, and films. Approximately 2 million people a year attend these events, while another two hundred thousand take guided tours of the complex.

The spectacular Sydney Opera House is one of Australia's most recognizable buildings.

Sydney's two-story Government House was the first brick building in the new colony. A common feature of later structures was a wide veranda, which provided shade and allowed air to circulate and cool off the inner rooms of the house. The need for plenty of ventilation was important in the tropical regions of the continent. In these areas, houses were often built on raised platforms supported by stilts, a style that came to be known as Queensland. Many consider this the most original local contribution to Australian architecture.

The most heralded architect of the day was Francis Greenway, a convict transported to the Australian penal colony. Sentenced to fourteen years for forgery, Greenway caught the attention of Governor Lachlan Macquarie, who appointed him civil architect in 1816. His Australian colonial style produced some of the most beautiful structures in the country. Examples of his work include the St. James's Church and Hyde Park Barracks in Sydney. Until recently, Greenway's portrait adorned Australian ten-dollar bills, a unique honor for a forger.

The Rialto Towers in Melbourne is the tallest office building in the Southern Hemisphere.

Although some tall buildings appeared in the 1920s, skyscrapers did not become popular until architect Harry Seidler arrived from Austria in 1948. Among his contributions are the 561-foot Australia Square tower, the MLC Centre, the Riverside Centre, and the QV1 Office Tower. The 830-foot Rialto Towers, built in 1986 by Australian developer Bruno Grollo, is the tallest office building in the entire Southern Hemisphere.

LITERATURE

The first Australian settlers described their experiences in oral songs and ballads, similar to the Aborigines. Some also kept journals recording their experiences, but it was not until about fifty years after the arrival of the First Fleet that a written Australian literature emerged. These first works were based on European models and intended for European audiences.

Poetry made its initial appearance on the continent in the early part of the nineteenth century. Englishman Barron Field's volume, *First Fruits of Australian Poetry,* was published in 1819. It was soon followed by "Australasia, an Ode," a poem by native-born Australian William Charles Westworth. This poem is generally recognized as the first to give voice to the spirit of Australian nationalism. The first native poet of significance was Henry Clarence Kendall, sometimes referred to as the Australian national poet. His works in the latter half of the century dealt with the unique features of the Australian landscape. His *Leaves from an Australian Forest* and *Songs from the Mountains* celebrate the scenery of the wooded valleys along the country's Pacific coast.

The best-known poet of the early twentieth century was A. B. "Banjo" Paterson. Paterson's bush ballads about outback life include "Waltzing Matilda," the unofficial song of Australia that was sung by Australian troops in both World War I and II. Some of his best works are included in his collection *The Man from Snowy River.* A poet with a more political inclination was Henry Lawson, whose "Song of the Republic" rallied the forces of Australian nationalism. Many of Paterson's and Lawson's works were first published in *The Bulletin,* the well-respected weekly literary newspaper founded by J. F. Archibald in 1880.

In more recent times, the work of Oodgeroo Noonuccal, the first Aboriginal to have a book of poetry published (*We Are Going,* 1964), has underscored the problems that Aboriginals face in a white society. As an activist, Noonuccal campaigned for the 1967 referendum that gave constitutional recognition to Aboriginals for the first time. For her contributions to society, she was made a member of the Order of the British Empire in 1970. Eighteen years later, however, she returned the honor to Queen Elizabeth II as a way of protesting the mistreatment of Aboriginals.

Early Australian fiction generally described the difficulties that the settlers faced in the harsh, foreign environment, and the Europeans' relations with the Aborigines. The first Australian novel was *Quintus Servinton* by Henry

Savery. Published in 1831, the autobiographical work describes the life of a convict in the colony. Charles Rowcroft is credited with producing the first work of fiction by a native Australian, *Tales of the Colonies,* in 1843. The most reputable of the early novelists was Henry Kingsley, who wrote about the rustic life of the period. *Such Is Life* (1903) by Thomas Furphy (writing as Tom Collins) is considered by some to be the greatest work of Australian fiction. The complex novel, written in diary form, is an episodic recounting of life in Australia in the 1880s. The era also produced Miles Franklin, one of Australia's early feminists, whose novel *My Brilliant Career* presented a look at outback life from a woman's point of view. It was later made into a highly acclaimed movie.

MODERN NOVELISTS

The twentieth century saw many other novels gain international acclaim. Frank Dalby Davison's *Man-Shy* (published in the United States as *Red Heifer*) describes life on a Queensland cattle station. *The Timeless Land* is Eleanor Dark's tale of the nation's founding told from the Aboriginal point of view. Ethel Florence Lindesay Richardson's trilogy, *The Fortunes of Richard Mahony,* looks at the Australian experience through the eyes of an unstable Irish doctor who intensely dislikes Australian life. The title character is considered one of the major creations of Australian literature.

The major figure among modern Australian novelists was Patrick White, who in 1973 became the first Australian to win a Nobel Prize in literature. His character studies have earned him a worldwide reputation. In *Tree of Man* (1954), White describes the loneliness of life in the bush country. His novel *Voss* (1957) relates the story of an unsuccessful attempt to penetrate the interior of the continent by a nineteenth-century German explorer.

In the late 1970s, Colleen McCullough topped the bestseller charts with *The Thorn Birds,* a saga of life in the outback that was later adapted for television. Thomas Keneally won the 1982 Booker Prize (awarded for the best full-length novel written by a citizen of the United Kingdom, the Commonwealth, Ireland, or South Africa) for his novel *Schindler's Ark.* It was later made into the highly praised movie *Schindler's List* by Steven Spielberg.

Acclaimed author Thomas Keneally wrote Schindler's Ark, *which was later adapted to the screen and retitled* Schindler's List.

MUSIC

Australian popular music of the last half century has followed trends begun in America and Great Britain. In the 1950s, Johnny O'Keefe, "Australia's King of Rock 'n' Roll," almost single-handedly established the Australian recording industry. His 1959 recording "Shout" became the country's rock 'n' roll national anthem.

The British sound of the sixties gave rise to the Seekers, the best-known Australian group of the period, who had several hits in England and America. In the 1970s, the Skyhooks was one of the foremost local bands, while the Bee Gees and the Little River Band were some of the first groups to gain worldwide attention. Popular solo artists included Helen Reddy, Rick Springfield, and Olivia Newton-John, who was born in England but moved to Australia when she was just five years old. In later years, Men at Work, INXS, and Kylie Minogue have had hits internationally.

Since 1990, Aboriginal music has become extremely popular. One of its leading proponents is Yothu Yindi (meaning "mother and child"), whose lead singer, Mandawuy Yunupingu, was named Australian of the Year in 1992. The group's recording "Treaty" was instrumental in popularizing the Aboriginal land rights movement.

Other types of music are also well received. Percy Grainger, Malcolm Williamson, and Alfred Hill are three composers who have achieved recognition outside of Australia. The country's leading proponent of jazz is unquestionably Don Burrows. Burrows plays the flute, clarinet, and saxophone, and was the first Australian jazz artist to earn a gold record. In the realm of opera, two well-known performers are Dame Nellie Melba (after whom the dessert Peach Melba is named) and Dame Joan Sutherland. The latter's husband, Richard Bonynge, has an international reputation as one of the country's top conductors.

Every Australian state and territory has its own symphony orchestra, managed by the Australian Broadcasting Corporation (ABC). The states also have opera and dance companies, among the best known of which are the Australian Ballet, the Victoria State Opera, and the Sydney Dance Company. Opera Australia, the national company, performs in the cities of Sydney and Melbourne.

A discussion of Australian music would not be complete without mention of two instruments native to the continent. The didgeridoo, perhaps the oldest instrument on Earth, is a long wooden flute made from tree limbs hollowed out by termites. Used as an accompaniment to Aboriginal chants and songs, it emits a low-pitched, resonant sound. Of more recent vintage is the lagerphone, a homemade instrument made of bottle tops that are loosely nailed to a stick. The tops rattle when the stick is hit or tapped. The lagerphone is generally associated with Australian folk music.

CINEMA

Australia has one of the world's oldest movie industries, dating back to 1896. That year, French photographer Maurice Sestier relocated to Sydney and began producing the nation's first films. Cinematic historians consider the religious epic *Soldiers of the Cross* to be the world's first feature-length film. It was produced in Australia in 1900. Another famous movie from the early years was *The Story of the Kelly Gang* (1906). Although over 250 features were produced in the silent film era, the industry began to decline in the 1920s when it was unable to compete with Hollywood's financial resources.

When movies featuring sound became popular in the 1930s, studios such as Cinesound came into existence. Many of the films produced were based on Australian history or literature. One of the most famous is *Forty Thousand Horsemen* (1940), the story of the Australian and New Zealand forces who fought German and Turkish troops in World War I. Another landmark film was *Jedda* (1957), the first to star an Aborigine, Robert Tudawali.

By the 1950s, Hollywood had become the film capital of the world. Australian filmmakers found it hard to compete with the Americans until the government stepped in around 1970 and began giving them subsidies. Since then, the industry has come into its own, producing many motion pictures that have gotten international recognition, including *Moulin Rouge, Picnic at Hanging Rock, The Man from Snowy River, Mad Max, The Year of Living Dangerously, Breaker Morant,* and *Crocodile Dundee.* Australian actors and directors of note include Errol Flynn, Cyril Ritchard, Nicole Kidman, Paul Hogan, Gillian Armstrong, Peter Weir, Bruce Beresford, and George Miller. Superstar Mel Gibson was born in Peekskill, New York, but grew up in Australia and attended the University of New South Wales.

SPORTS AND RECREATION

Although Australians enjoy going to the movies, they delight in participatory activities even more. Since they live in a nation with a warm climate and hundreds of beautiful beaches, it is only natural that Australians have a passionate love affair with sports, particularly water sports. Swimming, surfing, boating, and yachting are among the most popular activities. Aussie swimmers have achieved worldwide recognition for their talents, especially at the Summer Olympic Games. Dawn Fraser dominated women's swimming in the 1950s, and one of the best of the current men's crop is Ian Thorpe, who won three gold and two silver medals at the 2000 Games in Sydney.

Perhaps the greatest moment in Australian sports history occurred on September 26, 1983, when the boat *Australia II,* skippered by John Bertrand, won the America's Cup. He defeated American yachtsmen for the first time in the race's 132-year history. The event drew so much attention that Prime Minister Bob Hawke went on television to excuse everyone who was late for work or school because of having stayed up late to watch the final day of racing.

TWO-UP

Gambling has been an important part of the Australian scene ever since the first settlers arrived. One of the most popular forms of wagering is on the game of Two-Up. The basic idea of the game is to toss two coins so that they both come up heads. The player, called the "spinner," uses a flat stick, called a "kip," to toss the coins. Players stand around in a circle making bets as to whether the coins will come up both heads or both tails. Nothing happens on an "odd" toss of one head and one tail, unless it comes up five consecutive times. The spinner continues to throw until he tosses either three pairs of heads, a pair of tails, or five odds. When he does, the next player in the circle takes over as spinner.

Two-Up was the favorite game played by members of the Australian armed forces during World War I and World War II. Therefore, it is legal to play the game outside of a casino on only one day a year: ANZAC Day, the Australian national day of remembrance that commemorates the Australians who gave their lives in the wars.

For those who prefer nonaquatic activities, golf and tennis are popular individual sports that can be played year-round because of the warm climate. Greg Norman, winner of two British Open and five Australian Open titles, is the best-known Australian golfer. Rod Laver, Ken Rosewall, Margaret Smith Court, and Lew Hoad are names familiar to all tennis fans. Evonne Goolagong Cawley, a Wiradjuri Aboriginal and winner of two Wimbledon and four Australian Open titles, was the first Aboriginal athlete to gain worldwide fame.

The most popular summer team sport is cricket, an English pastime related to baseball. It was brought to the colony by the early settlers. Five-day-long test (international) matches have been held between Australia and England since 1877. Over the years, the sport has helped strengthen national feelings, since it was one of the few areas in which Australia could compete on an even level with the mother country. Sir Donald Bradman, universally acclaimed as the greatest cricketer of all time, was a native of New South Wales, where the Bradman Museum now stands.

Australian Rules Football (footy) draws the most attention in winter, outdrawing soccer by an appreciable margin. It

The crew of Australia II *celebrates after defeating their American competitors in the final race of the America's Cup in 1983.*

was invented in Victoria in the 1850s and is a cross between soccer, rugby, and Gaelic football. The championship game, called the Grand Final, is comparable to the Super Bowl in the United States.

Footy has been around for more than a century and a half, but it is not Australia's oldest sport. That designation is usually reserved for horse racing. Racetracks can be found everywhere you go. As English novelist Anthony Trollope wrote in the 1870s, "There is hardly a town to be called a town which has not its racecourse, and there are many racecourses where there are no towns."[14] The first official race was run outside of Sydney in 1810. The day of the Melbourne Cup—the country's most prestigious thoroughbred race that has been held annually since 1861—is a national holiday when many schools and businesses close their doors. Phar Lap, Australia's most famous racehorse and arguably the greatest racehorse ever, is the only horse to have been the favorite for the Melbourne Cup three years in a row. His stuffed

SURF LIFESAVING

Since the majority of Australia's 19 million people live within an hour or two of the beach, swimming, surfing, and other water sports are the nation's most popular pastimes. With such an emphasis on beach activity, it is understandable that water safety is an important concern. Many of Australia's eight thousand beaches are patrolled by Surf Life Saving Australia (SLSA), one of the largest volunteer organizations in the world. As set forth on its website, SLSA's mission is "to provide a safe beach and aquatic environment throughout Australia." It does so by providing a variety of services, including traditional beach patrols, school education programs, offshore rescue boat services, and a medical research program.

SLSA has over eighty-two thousand members representing 269 surf lifesaving clubs across the country. Anyone from age seven and up can join to learn the skills necessary to become a lifesaver. Youngsters from ages seven to thirteen become Nippers and start learning about water safety. At age thirteen, they can become probationary surf lifesavers. Anyone over the age of fifteen can obtain the Bronze Medallion, which is the minimum qualification necessary for beach patrol.

Protecting the public by helping to prevent accidents before they occur is the most important skill taught to lifesavers. The rescue of people is the second most important skill. Although there is no way to know how many accidents have been prevented, the number of rescues performed by SLSA members is approaching the half million mark.

Surf Life Saving Australia volunteers (seen here in a surf rescue boat) have performed nearly a half million rescues.

body is on display in the Australia Gallery at Melbourne Museum.

One of the highlights of the 2000 sports season was the Summer Olympic Games held in Sydney. More than ten thousand athletes from around the world competed in what International Olympic Committee president Juan Antonio Samaranch called "the best Olympic Games ever."[15] Australia garnered fifty-eight medals, including sixteen gold, to finish fourth in the medal standings. The nation was also host to the 1956 Games in Melbourne.

Australian athletes are beginning to make their presence felt in American professional sports leagues. Luc Longley, the first Aussie to play in the National Basketball Association, was a member of the championship Chicago Bulls teams of 1996, 1997, and 1998. Perhaps the best-known major league baseball player from Australia is catcher Dave Nilsson, who played for the Milwaukee Brewers from 1992 to 1999.

Australia's Challenges and Concerns

Most Australians consider their nation the best country on earth. However, like any other country, Australia has specific issues to address and decisions to make as it faces the future. Some of these, like preserving the environment and fending off global warming, are of relatively recent origin. Others, like the plight of the Aboriginals, have been a topic of debate for decades. These problems cannot be ignored if Australia is to keep improving its standing as a member of the global community. Whether to face them as a republic or a commonwealth of the British Empire is a primary concern.

Commonwealth or Republic?

For the last quarter of the twentieth century, the debate about Australia's national identity has been a major issue. On one side are the republicans, who want the country to cut all ties with Great Britain and to place an Australian at the head of state. On the opposite side are the monarchists, who want Australia to continue as a commonwealth of Great Britain.

Republicans argue that immigration over the past fifty years has completely changed the cultural makeup of the nation. With the British segment of the population no longer the overwhelming majority, there is no reason, they say, for Britain's monarch to be the head of state. Monarchists, on the other hand, believe the current system has served the nation well, and there is no good reason to change.

In 1986, the Australia Act was passed, breaking all legislative ties with Britain, but still keeping the queen as sovereign. When Paul Keating and the Labor Party were in power in the early 1990s, it appeared that it would be only a matter of time until Australia established itself as a republic. However, when

COMPULSORY VOTING

The government of Australia was one of the first in the world to institute a policy of compulsory voting among its citizens. The procedure was adopted in Queensland in 1915, and established nationwide in 1924. The stated purpose of the measure was to eliminate voter apathy and to ensure that elections reflected the will of the entire electorate. Opponents of the action say it is an infringement upon their rights.

In reality, the law does little more than ensure that citizens show up at the polling place. Since Australia uses a secret ballot, it is impossible to know who carries through on his or her voting responsibility. Many people register what is called an "informal" vote by marking their ballot improperly, or not marking it at all. Others respond with "donkey" votes in which they simply number the candidates in the order in which they appear on the ballot.

Compulsory voting is not nearly as rigid as it may sound. Citizens can get around the law by simply failing to register when moving to a new address. Even when a registered voter does not show up, the penalties are not severe. An excuse of sickness or a sudden emergency is often accepted by electoral officials. For the very small percentage of people found guilty of failing to vote, the punishment is generally no more than a fine of twenty dollars.

John Howard became prime minister in 1996, the prospects dimmed as Howard admitted to being a monarchist. He eventually agreed to set up a constitutional convention to meet and consider the question.

On February 13, 1998, the convention voted overwhelmingly in favor of severing ties with the British monarchy. The country was to become a republic on January 1, 2001, the one hundredth anniversary of confederation. The convention's 152 delegates came up with a model for a republic headed by a president chosen by the prime minister. This model was placed before the electorate in a 1999 referendum. Unfortunately, the majority of Australians in favor of a republic wanted the president chosen by direct election of the voters. When the votes were counted, the Australian Capital Territory was the only region that voted for a republic. Although the republican movement is still very much alive, any change in the status quo in the immediate future is unlikely.

ABORIGINE LAND RIGHTS

Many hope there will be a change in the status quo with regard to the rights of Aboriginal peoples. This segment of the population has been looked down upon as second-class citizens until relatively recently. Much work remains to be done in the field of Aboriginal rights, particularly concerning the land itself.

When the British came to Australia in the eighteenth century, they claimed the land under the legal principle of *terra nullius,* meaning the land was legally unoccupied. According to that reasoning, they could take the land without offering any sort of compensation. The concept of land ownership was foreign to the Aboriginals, who believed that people belonged to the land rather than the other way around. It was not until after World War II that the question of land rights for Aboriginals became an issue.

Delegates to a constitutional convention in Canberra applaud after overwhelmingly voting to sever Australia's 210-year link to the British monarchy in 1988.

In 1962, the Yolngu people of Yirrkala in Arnhem Land went to court demanding that the government recognize the Aboriginals' occupation and ownership of Australia. They lost the case, as the court upheld the principle of *terra nullius*. Because of the decision's racist implications, however, pressure was put on the government to make some provision for Aboriginal land rights. The eventual outcome was the Aboriginal Land Rights (Northern Territory) Act of 1976.

Over the next decade, a series of such acts gave Aboriginals limited claims to lands in certain regions. In the Northern Territory, for example, claimable land was only that which was outside local town boundaries—in other words, land that no one else owned or wanted. A claim for the sacred site of Uluru was disallowed because the land lay within the boundaries of a national park.

In 1982, five Torres Strait Islanders, led by Edward Koiki Mabo, filed a land claim suit against the Queensland government. They argued that their people had ancestral rights to land that had been taken from them on Murray Island. After a ten-year battle, the High Court ruled that Aboriginals could indeed hold title to lands to which they had a long-term link (native title). This ruling was important, since it invalidated the concept of *terra nullius*. Known as the Mabo decision, it is one of the most controversial rulings ever handed down in an Australian court of law.

In 1993, Parliament passed the Native Title Act to clarify the principle of native title. Guidelines were set to reassure farmers and miners that Aboriginals could not lay claim to the entire continent. They could only lay claim to lands that no one else owned or leased, and to which they had a long-time physical association. The ruling also set out a means of compensating Aboriginals whose native title had been lost.

The effect of the Native Title Act is open to debate, and several amendments have since been proposed. In the 1993 Wik case, the court ruled that native title to land under pastoral lease (in which the government leases the land to a farmer for a long period of time) was not lost, and could, in fact, exist at the same time as the lease. In case of a conflict, however, the pastoral lease would take precedence.

Aboriginal rights were further limited by the government's 1997 Ten Point Plan that eliminated native title under certain conditions. The plan was incorporated in the Native Title

THE STOLEN GENERATION

One of the black marks in Australian history was revealed in 1995 when the federal attorney general's office established the National Inquiry into the Separation of Aboriginal and Torres Strait Islander Children from Their Families. For many, it was the first indication they had that local governments had been taking a "stolen generation" of Aboriginal children from their parents for more than sixty years.

As far back as the early nineteenth century, Australian authorities instituted policies that tried to instill Aboriginals with British culture. Many families were removed to reserves, where they were controlled by white managers. When they found children being raised in what they considered substandard conditions, they removed them to orphanages. Many of the children remained in these homes until they were teenagers. Others were placed in homes with white families. As many as one hundred thousand children were taken from their natural parents in this way.

In 1997, the Human Rights and Equal Opportunity Commission published their report, "Bringing Them Home," based on the results of the inquiry. The report called for a government apology, compensation to Aboriginal families, and a national Sorry Day. On August 26, 1999, the federal Parliament passed a historic declaration expressing deep regret for these past injustices to the Aboriginals.

Amendment Bill of 1997, which strictly limits Aboriginal rights, leaving them with little to say about how leased and reserved lands can be used. Possibly the only thing that is clear is that the land rights battle is not yet over.

CREATURES IN JEOPARDY

The Aboriginals were not the only inhabitants of the land to be affected by the arrival of the Europeans. Australia must also address the extinction and endangerment of many of its unique species. Changes to the landscape as a result of human activity have already rendered many of these plants and animals extinct, and others find their survival threatened. Extinction is a definite future possibility for much of Australia's precious wildlife unless measures to prevent it are taken.

It is estimated that thirteen species of mammals and one bird species have become extinct since the settlement of Australia by the Europeans. Many others are now considered endangered. Some species have suffered because the range of their natural habitat has been reduced. Grasslands, for example, have been affected by clearing for pastures and crops. Others, such as the crocodile, koala, ringtail possum, and seal, have been reduced in number because of commercial hunting.

Many scientists have debated the role the Aboriginals have played. Many large animals (megafauna) were on the continent when the first Aboriginals arrived from Asia. These included the giant short-faced kangaroos (*Sthenurus* and *Procoptodon*), the giant wombat (*Phascolonus*), the marsupial lion (*Thylacoleo*), giant flightless birds (*Genyornis*), and the *Diprotodon*, a plant-eating mammal as large as a rhinoceros. Whether these extinctions were the result of Aboriginal hunting or environmental changes is a matter of conjecture.

Some damage to the environment has been caused by the introduction—both intentional and accidental—of other species. The most famous case of such an instance was the legendary rabbit infestation. In 1859, Thomas Austin imported twenty-four wild rabbits from England and released them on his property in southern Victoria for sport hunting. The rabbits spread quickly in such large numbers that their movement across the landscape was referred to as a "grey blanket." As crops became devastated, the New South Wales Parliament voted in favor of the animals' eradication. Financial rewards were offered to whoever captured or killed any of the pests. Fences were constructed to keep the animals away from crops, but without much success.

Because of the competition for food, the rabbit was displacing many small- and medium-sized animals, and was changing the ecosystem. Other animals were also killed by poisons and traps that were intended for the rabbits. In addition, because the rabbits were eating the vegetation cover, the underlying soil was degraded.

In 1887, the government offered a large reward to whoever could come up with a biological method that would effectively destroy the rabbits. It was not until 1950, however, that a partial solution was found. That year, myxomatosis, a dis-

ease transmitted by fleas and mosquitoes, was introduced into Australia by the Commonwealth Scientific and Industrial Research Organisation (CSIRO). Within two years, the rabbit population was reduced from 600 million to less than 100 million. The solution worked for about twenty years until the rabbits developed an immunity to the virus. The government is currently trying to control the rabbit population using immunocontraception, whereby gene insertion of a virus makes the animal infertile. The hope is that by using a combination of these methods, the rabbit population will be kept under control and the damage to the environment halted.

New South Wales residents drive hundreds of rabbits into a pen. The rabbit infestation problem, which began in 1859, continues today.

THE THREAT OF GLOBAL WARMING

Nowadays, the reality of global warming is no longer questioned by most world governments. Since the beginning of the industrial age, the elevated carbon dioxide levels in the atmosphere have been primarily responsible for a rise in the global sea level from ten to twenty-five centimeters. Sea ice in the Antarctic has shrunk southward, and ice caps on some of the world's tallest mountains are beginning to disappear. As CSIRO research scientist Graeme Pearman said, "The debate about whether it's going to happen is well and truly over. Most questions remaining are about what people are going to do."[16]

Because of its low land and high temperatures, the United Nations' intergovernmental panel on climate change identified Australia as the country likely to be the most affected among the nations of the industrialized world if the warming trend continues. The latest scenarios developed by CSIRO describe some of the possible change outcomes that could result.

The CSIRO projections suggest that further temperature rises of as much as six degrees Celsius could occur by the year 2070. (An average increase of only four to six degrees Celsius was enough to thaw out the most recent ice age.) The highest increases would take place in the inland regions and along the northern coast.

The change in temperature would likely produce several effects. Winter rainfall might decrease as much as 20 percent over most of the Australian mainland. Much of the polar ice caps would melt, causing a further rise in the level of the oceans. This could result in frequent coastal flooding, more severe coastal erosion, and higher storm surges. The winter snow cover in the Great Dividing Range would melt, affecting both plant and animal communities.

The increased heat could result in a decrease in relative humidity and a greater risk of fires in much of Australia. This, in turn, could have a substantial effect on the plant life in the affected regions. Drought-tolerant species would likely thrive at the expense of grasses in the semi-arid grasslands.

Insect and animal life would also be affected. Some species, like the cattle tick and Queensland fruit fly, could migrate farther south. An increase in temperature might increase the number of insect generations produced in a year, leading to more serious pest-control problems. With water and plant life harder to come by, animals might be forced to migrate from their natural habitats. Those that did not adapt would have their very existence threatened.

In addition to the environmental impact of global warming, there would also be a socioeconomic one as well. Not

THE CANE TOAD

By past experience, Australians have become well aware of the dangers involved in introducing exotic species of animals into new habitats. The animal will often cause more problems than it was brought in to resolve. The cane toad is one example of such an animal.

The cane toad (*Bufo marinus*) was introduced to Australia from Venezuela in 1935. It was intentionally brought to the northeast coast at Gordonvale, North Queensland. Despite warnings by scientists and naturalists, they were brought in by the Australian Bureau of Sugar Experimental Stations to eat cane beetles that were damaging the sugar cane harvest. Unfortunately, the toads did not solve the beetle problem, but instead caused one of their own.

The six-inch-long toads have a variable diet and thus do not have much difficulty finding food. They quickly adapted to their new environment and flourished. The female of the species can produce as many as thirty thousand eggs a month. The toads soon spread throughout Queensland, into the Northern Territory and New South Wales.

As the warty-skinned amphibians spread over the land, they caused unexpected problems. Although the cane toad looks harmless enough, its skin contains glands that secrete a deadly poison. Many of the country's predators ate the animal and died. Since the toads' expansion has not yet been halted, the amount of damage they have caused is yet to be determined.

The cane toad was originally imported to Australia as a pest control agent for sugar cane crops, but the poison secreted by the toad proved to be deadly to its predators.

the least of these would be the effect on the health of Australians. The increase of allergens and air pollution would affect the incidence of respiratory diseases, while the spread of the insect population could lead to an increase of mosquito-borne diseases such as Australian encephalitis, Ross River fever, and dengue.

The spread of flood damage due to more severe coastal storms and water runoff from the mountains might necessitate increased spending on dams and drainage systems. Additional funds might be needed for repairs to roads, bridges, and railways. Coastal regions would probably require funding to protect local buildings and industries. Any damage—or threats of future damage—would also have major implications for the insurance industry.

The economic effects on tourism would also be significant. Millions of dollars of revenue would be lost because of damage to beach and resort areas. Reduction of snow cover in the mountain region and an increased risk of contracting serious diseases would also reduce the number of potential tourists.

The serious implications of global warming can no longer be taken lightly. As more and more studies are made, one thing is becoming certain: the longer the problem is ignored, the more dire the consequences will be.

THE VANISHING RAIN FOREST

Despite its status as the driest of the inhabited continents, Australia is also home to one of the world's most beautiful, and ecologically significant, rain forests. Unfortunately, as in other parts of the world, Australia's rain forest is in danger of being destroyed. The area in question, known as the Wet Tropics World Heritage Rainforest, is located along the northeast coast of Queensland, extending from south of Cooktown to north of Townsville. Palms, ferns, and vines grow in abundance among the oaks, cedar, brush box, and beeches. The region is subject to a high annual rainfall that is concentrated within a four-month period.

In the two hundred years since Europeans arrived on the continent, nearly 75 percent of the Australian rain forest has been lost or drastically altered. The rain forest is home to hundreds of species of animal and plant life, including many that are restricted to the region. Although the area represents

only about one one-thousandth of the continent's surface, approximately 62 percent of Australia's butterfly species, 60 percent of its bat species, 30 percent of its marsupial and frog species, 23 percent of its reptile species, and 18 percent of its bird species can be found in the rain forest. This biodiversity is being threatened because of modification of the environment. Over 350 varieties of plants and 35 species of animals that are found there are regarded as rare, threatened, or endangered.

Since Edmund Kennedy and George Elphinstone Dalrymple explored this part of Queensland in 1848 and 1873, respectively, outside forces have been damaging the ecosystem. Trees have been cut down for timber, and land has been cleared away for cane plantations. (Other plans for roads, airports, and reservoirs have also been considered but thus far avoided.) This leads, in turn, to problems such as soil erosion and an increase in the amount of greenhouse-gas emissions. Tin mining in the region has also had an unfavorable impact

The Australian rain forest, which is home to hundreds of species of animal and plant life, is in danger of being destroyed.

on the rain forest, as has tourism, to a degree. Another factor of the rain forest's destruction has been the introduction of new plants and animals, and the diseases they carry. One example is the *Thunbergia grandiflora,* a woody vine introduced from India that has caused the death of some trees.

Although Australia lacks a coordinated approach to environmental management, several organizations are working toward that goal. Among these are Greening Australia and Landcare. The Queensland Wet Tropics World Heritage Protection and Management Act of 1993 and the Commonwealth Wet Tropics of Queensland World Heritage Area Conservation Act of 1994 provide guidelines for the area's protection. The government's One Billion Trees program is also a step in the right direction.

Despite these problems, Australia has made tremendous progress since its settlement as a British colony just over two hundred years ago. With hard work and an ability to laugh at themselves, Australians face the twenty-first century optimistically. As Donald Horne wrote in *The Lucky Country,* they stand tall, "delighting in life for its vigour and activity, without asking questions about it."[17]

FACTS ABOUT AUSTRALIA

AUSTRALIA

Official name: Commonwealth of Australia.

Form of government: federal parliamentary state (formally a constitutional monarchy) with two legislative houses (Senate [76]; House of Representatives [148]).

Chief of state: British monarch represented by governor-general.

Head of government: prime minister.

Capital: Canberra.

Official language: English.

Official religion: none.

Monetary unit: 1 Australian dollar ($A)=100 cents; valuation (Nov. 21, 2001) 1 U.S.$=$A 1.93.

DEMOGRAPHY

Population (1997): 18,508,000.

Density (1997): persons per square mile 6.2, persons per square kilometer 2.4.

Urban-rural (1996): urban 85.0%; rural 15.0%.

Sex distribution (1996): male 49.46%; female 50.54%.

Age breakdown (1996): under 15, 21.6%; 15–24, 14.5%; 25–44, 30.8%; 45–64, 21.0%; 65 and over, 12.1%.

Population projection: (2000) 19,058,000; (2010) 20,830,000.

Doubling time: 99 years.

Ethnic composition (1996): white 95.2%; Aboriginal 2.0%; Asian 1.3%; other 1.5%.

Religious affiliation (1991): Christian 74.0%, of which Roman Catholic 27.3%, Anglican Church of Australia 23.8%, other Protestant 20.1% (Uniting Church and Methodist 8.2%, Presbyterian 4.3%), Orthodox 2.8%; Muslim 0.9%; Buddhist 0.8%; Jewish 0.4%; no religion 12.9%; other 11.0%.

Major cities (1995): Sydney 3,772,700; Melbourne 3,218,100; Brisbane 1,489,100; Perth 1,262,600; Adelaide 1,081,000; Newcastle 466,000; Canberra-Queanbeyan 331,800; Gold Coast–Tweed 326,900; Wollongong 253,600; Hobart 194,700.

Place of birth (1996): 73.9% native-born; 26.1% foreign-born, of which Europe 12.4% (United Kingdom 6.3%, Italy 1.3%, Greece 0.7%, Germany 0.6%, The Netherlands 0.5%, other Europe 3.0%), Asia and Middle East 5.6%, New Zealand 1.6%, Africa, the Americas, and other 6.5%.

Mobility (1995–96): population age 15 and over living in the same residence as in 1994: 81.6%; different residence between states, regions, and neighborhoods 18.4%.

Households (1993–94): total number of households 6,616,800. Average household size 2.6; one person 21.8%, couples only 25.8%, couples with dependent children only 23.7%, nonfamily members 12.4%, single parent with children 6.6%, other 9.7%.

Immigration (1996): permanent immigrants admitted 96,970, from United Kingdom and Ireland 12.8%, New Zealand 11.8%, China 7.6%, Vietnam 4.8%, Hong Kong 4.6%, India 4.4%, Philippines 3.9%, South Africa 3.2%, Bosnia and Herzegovina 3.2%, Yugoslavia 3.1%, Sri Lanka 2.2%. Refugee arrivals (1994–95): 13,600.

VITAL STATISTICS

Birthrate per 1,000 population (1996): 14.1 (world average 25.0); (1993) legitimate 75.0%; illegitimate 25.0%.

Death rate per 1,000 population (1996): 6.9 (world average 9.3).

Natural increase rate per 1,000 population (1996): 7.2 (world average 15.7).

Total fertility rate (average births per childbearing woman; 1996): 1.82.

Marriage rate per 1,000 population (1996): 6.0.

Divorce rate per 1,000 population (1996): 2.7.

Life expectancy at birth (1996): male 75.4 years; female 81.1 years.

Major causes of death per 100,000 population (1995): diseases of the circulatory system 296.0; cancers 190.0; respiratory diseases 52.0; accidents, poisoning, and violence 41.0; endocrine, nutritional, and metabolic diseases 23.0; digestive system diseases 21.0; nervous system diseases 17.0.

SOCIAL INDICATORS

Educational attainment (1995). Percentage of population age 15 to 64 having: no formal schooling 0.3%; incomplete secondary education 36.3%; completed secondary 17.8; postsecondary, technical, or other certificate/diploma 33.7%; university 11.9%.

Quality of working life (1995–96). Average workweek: 40.5 hours (16.8% overtime). Annual rate per 100,000 workers for: accidental injury and industrial disease, 3,200; death, n.a. Proportion of employed persons insured for damages or income loss resulting from: injury 100%; permanent disability 100%; death 100%. Working days lost to industrial disputes per 1,000 employees (1995): 79. Means of transportation to work (1986): private automobile 69.4%; public transportation 10.1%; motorcycle and bicycle 3.2%; foot 6.6%; other 10.7%. Discouraged job seekers (considered by employers to be too young or too old, having language or training limitations, or no vacancies in line of work; 1995): 1.3% of labor force.

Access to services (1976). Proportion of dwellings having access to: electricity 99.5%; bathroom 96.0%; flush toilet 92.2%; kitchen 97.9%; public sewer 73.4%.

Social participation. Eligible voters participating in last national election (1996): 95.8%; voting is compulsory. Population age 16 and over participating in voluntary work: n.a. Trade union membership in total workforce (1996): 31%.

Social deviance (1996). Offense rate per 100,000 population for: murder 3.8; sexual assault 78.7; assault 620.8; auto theft 672.2; unarmed robbery, burglary, and housebreaking 4,608.2; armed robbery 34.0. Incidence per 100,000 in general population of: alcoholism, n.a.; prisoners with drug offenses (1994) 8.8; suicide (1995) 13.1.

Material well-being (1995). Households possessing: automobile 85%; telephone 95%; refrigerator 99.7%; air conditioner 32.3%; personal computer 23.0%; washing machine 90.0%; central heating 3.9%; swimming pool 10.1%.

ECONOMY

Gross national product (1995): U.S.$337,909,000,000 (U.S.$18,720 per capita).

Budget (1996–97). Revenue: $A 130,160,000,000 (income tax 71.2%, of which individual 50.7%, corporate 15.1%; excise duties and sales tax 21.0%). Expenditures: $A 129,686,000,000 (social security and welfare 37.7%; health 15.0%; economic and public services 12.7%; transfers to state governments 12.9%; interest on public debt 7.5%).

Public debt (1996): $A 97,659,000,000.

Tourism (1996): receipts from visitors U.S.$8,127,500,000; expenditures by nationals abroad U.S.$5,038,800,000.

Household income and expenditure (1993–94). Average household size 2.6; average annual income per household $A 37,700 (U.S.$27,585); sources of income: wages and salaries 72.7%, transfer payments 13.0%, self-employment 7.5%, other 6.8%; expenditure: food and beverages 18.7%, transportation and communications 15.3%, housing 13.9%, recreation 13.3%, household durable goods 6.6%, clothing and footwear 5.7%, health 4.6%, energy 2.8%, other 19.1%.

Imports (1995–96): $A 77,819,000,000 (machinery 33.4%, of which office machines and automatic data-processing equipment 7.7%; basic manufactures 14.2%, of which textile yarn and fabrics 3.0%, paper and paper products 2.5%, iron and steel 1.8%; transport equipment 13.5%, of which road motor vehicles 10.2%; chemicals and related products 11.4%; mineral fuels and lubricants 5.5%; food and live animals 3.7%; crude materials [inedible] excluding fuels 2.0%; beverages and tobacco 0.6%).

Major import sources: U.S. 22.6%; Japan 13.9%; U.K. 6.3%; Germany 6.2%; China 5.1%.

Exports (1995–96): $A 75,999,000,000 (food and live animals 20.1%, of which cereals and cereal preparations 6.5%, meat and meat preparations 4.3%, sugar, sugar preparations, and honey 2.3%, dairy products 2.2%; crude materials excluding fuels 19.4%, of which metalliferous ores and metal scrap 11.4%, textile fibers and their waste 5.3%; mineral fuels and lubricants 16.6%, of which coal, coke, and briquettes 10.3%, petroleum, petroleum products, and natural gas 4.2%; basic manufactures 12.9%).

Major export destinations: Japan 21.6%; South Korea 8.7%; New Zealand 7.4%; U.S. 6.0%; China 5.0%; Singapore 4.7%; Taiwan 4.5%; Hong Kong 4.0%.

NOTES

INTRODUCTION: GODZONE

1. Quoted in Elizabeth Hansen, *Frommer's Australia*. New York: Macmillan Travel, 1996, p. 24.

CHAPTER 1: THE LAND DOWN UNDER

2. Quoted in Hansen, *Frommer's Australia*, p. 341.

CHAPTER 2: THE FIRST AUSTRALIANS

3. Quoted in Roderick Cameron, *Australia: History and Horizons*. New York: Columbia University Press, 1971, p. 23.

4. Quoted in Cameron, *Australia: History and Horizons*, p. 50.

5. Quoted in Hansen, *Frommer's Australia*, p. 142.

6. Quoted in John H. Chambers, *A Traveller's History of Australia*. New York: Interlink Books, 1999, p. 56.

7. Quoted in Stuart Macintyre, *A Concise History of Australia*. Cambridge: Cambridge University Press, 1999, p. 28.

CHAPTER 3: FEDERATION AND BEYOND

8. Quoted in Macintyre, *A Concise History of Australia*, p. 52.

9. Quoted in Cameron, *Australia: History and Horizons*, p. 164.

10. Quoted in Sonja B. Starr, ed., *Let's Go Australia 1999*. New York: St. Martin's Press, 1999, p. 54.

11. Quoted in Macintyre, *A Concise History of Australia*, p. 220.

CHAPTER 4: THE AUSTRALIAN WAY OF LIFE

12. Quoted in Hansen, *Frommer's Australia*, p. 474.

CHAPTER 5: AUSTRALIAN CULTURE: A MIXTURE OF OLD AND NEW

13. Quoted in Cameron, *Australia: History and Horizons*, pp. 245–46.

14. Quoted in Chambers, *A Traveller's History of Australia*, p. 191.

15. Quoted in Ted Anthony, "Sydney Olympic Games End," *AP Online*, October 2, 2000. special.northernlight.com/olympics/end.htm.

Chapter 6: Australia's Challenges and Concerns

16. Quoted in Amanda Hodge, "Act Now to Keep Your Cool," *The Australian*, July 20, 2001. www.theaustralian.news.com.au/common/story_page/0,5744,2515052%255E14769,00.html.

17. Quoted in Hansen, *Frommer's Australia*, p. 6.

GLOSSARY

Aborigine: one of the native Australians, of whom only 160,000 are left in the country.

barbie: a barbecue.

billabong: small pool left behind when a river dries up.

bush: rural area, backcountry.

bushrangers: bandits who lived in the bush (many were escaped convicts), held up travelers, and ransacked isolated homes.

didgeridoo: a long, hollow wind instrument.

dingo: wild dog.

footy: Australian Rules Football.

marsupial: derived from the Latin word for "pouch," a marsupial is a type of mammal that carries its young in a pouch. Marsupials found in Australia include kangaroos and koalas.

mate: a best buddy.

monotremes: egg-laying mammals.

outback: land not in the cities, belonging to the bush.

snorkers: sausages.

trepang: variety of sea cucumber.

woomera: spear-thrower.

CHRONOLOGY

40,000–50,000 B.C.
Aboriginal tribes arrive in Australia.

A.D. **150**
Greek philosopher Ptolemy predicts the existence of Australia and calls it *terra australis incognita* (the unknown southern land).

1606
Captain Willem Jansz sights Australia.

1616–1619
Dutch explore the Australian coast.

1642
Abel Janszoon Tasman sights Van Diemen's Land (Tasmania).

1688
William Dampier becomes the first Englishman to land in Australia.

1768
Captain James Cook leaves England in *Endeavour* and sails to the South Pacific.

1770
Captain Cook claims New South Wales for Great Britain.

1788
Captain Arthur Phillip and the First Fleet land at Botany Bay; British penal colony established in New South Wales; Sydney founded.

1790
The Second Fleet (the Rum Corps) arrives.

1793
First school opens in Sydney.

1794
Captain Macarthur starts the sheep-breeding industry.

99

1796
Matthew Flinders explores coastline aboard *Tom Thumb*.

1797
Coal found in New South Wales.

1801–1803
Matthew Flinders circumnavigates Australia.

1813
Explorers George Blaxland, William Wentworth, and William Lawson find a way through the Blue Mountains. Settlement of the interior begins.

1824
Brisbane founded.

1829
Britain lays claim to the entire continent; Captain Charles Fremantle claims Western Australia for Great Britain; Perth founded.

1835
Melbourne is founded by John Pascoe Fawkner and John Batman.

1836
Adelaide founded.

1841
Edward John Eyre travels from South Australia to Western Australia.

1844
Ludwig Leichhardt explores 2,000 miles (3,219 kilometers) of Australia from Brisbane to the Gulf of Carpentaria.

1845
Copper discovered in South Australia.

1850
University of Sydney established.

1851
Gold is discovered in Victoria and New South Wales. Victoria separates from New South Wales.

1855
Van Diemen's Land renamed Tasmania in honor of Abel Tasman.

1859
Queensland separates from New South Wales.

1868
Great Britain stops sending convicts to Australia.

1872
First international telegraph line is completed from Port Darwin to Banjoewanji, Indonesia.

1891
Australia's constitution is drafted.

1894
Women receive the right to vote.

1898
Federal constitution is written.

1901
Australia declared an independent commonwealth.

1909
Australian navy is created.

1914
Australia enters World War I.

1915
Australian and New Zealand Army Corps (ANZAC) formed on April 25 (date now celebrated as ANZAC Day); more than eight thousand Australian soldiers are lost in the battle at Gallipoli.

1920
Qantas Airways founded.

1923
Radio broadcasting begins.

1925
Compulsory voting begins.

1927
Canberra becomes the capital of Australia.

1928
The Royal Flying Doctor Service begins in Alice Springs.

1930–1935
Great Depression felt in Australia.

1939
Australia enters World War II.

1952
Uranium ore discovered in South Australia and Northern Territory.

1963
Aboriginals given full rights as citizens.

1965
Australian troops sent to Vietnam.

1966
United States requests and receives additional troop support from Australia in Vietnam.

1967
Federal aid programs started for Aboriginals.

1973
Sydney Opera House is completed.

1974
Cyclone Tracy strikes Darwin.

1976
Aboriginal Land Rights Act passed.

1983
Australia II wins the America's Cup.

1988
Australia celebrates bicentennial.

1993
A compromise plan for Aboriginal land claims is unveiled that will validate certain claims and provide government compensation for nullified claims; Mandawuy Yunupingu, an Aboriginal music performer of the group Yothu Yindi, is chosen Australian of the Year; Prime Minister Keating announces that Australia will become a republic by the year 2001, subject to approval by referendum.

1999
Referendum on plan to become a republic voted down.

SUGGESTIONS FOR FURTHER READING

BOOKS

Bill Bryson, *In a Sunburned Country.* New York: Broadway Books, 2000. An entertaining account of the author's travels through the island continent.

Laura Dolce, *Australia.* New York: Chelsea House Publishers, 1990. This volume in the Places and Peoples of the World series is an easy-to-read history of Australia, with an emphasis on modern-day life.

Virginia Luling, *Aborigines.* London: Macdonald Educational, 1979. This book in the Surviving Peoples series for young people is a richly illustrated look at Australia's original inhabitants.

Geoffrey Moorhouse, *Sydney: The Story of a City.* New York: Harcourt, 1999. The story of Australia's first city, the site of the 2000 Summer Olympics.

Ross Terrill, *The Australians.* New York: Simon and Schuster, 1987. A native Australian paints a picture of the fascinating "Land Down Under" and its inhabitants.

Lynne Withey, *Voyages of Discovery.* New York: William Morrow and Company, 1987. The story of Captain James Cook and his exploration of the Pacific.

WORKS CONSULTED

BOOKS

Roderick Cameron, *Australia: History and Horizons.* New York: Columbia University Press, 1971. A detailed history of Australia, with numerous illustrations, from the time of the arrival of the first Europeans.

John H. Chambers, *A Traveller's History of Australia.* New York: Interlink Books, 1999. This book gives a complete account of the history of Australia and its amazing diversity. Included is a historical gazetteer that highlights the chief places of interest for tourists.

Miriam Estensen, *Discovery: The Quest for the Great South Land.* New York: St. Martin's Press, 1998. This volume relates the story of the search for the sixth continent.

Elizabeth Hansen, *Frommer's Australia.* New York: Macmillan Travel, 1996. This annual guide presents a comprehensive listing of sights to be seen in the Land Down Under.

Mary Ann Harrell, *Surprising Lands Down Under.* Washington: National Geographic Society, 1989. Lavishly illustrated, this book provides a look at life in Australia and New Zealand through the eyes of its inhabitants.

Robert Hughes, *The Fatal Shore.* New York: Alfred A. Knopf, 1987. A detailed account of the birth of Australia out of England's infamous convict transportation system.

Stuart Macintyre, *A Concise History of Australia.* Cambridge: Cambridge University Press, 1999. This volume details the history of Australia, relating how the Europeans have replaced the old with the new over the past two hundred years.

John Rickard, *Australia: A Cultural History.* New York: Addison Wesley Longman, 1996. This book tells the story of Australia through an examination of its evolving values, beliefs, rites, and customs.

Sonja B. Starr, ed., *Let's Go Australia 1999*. New York: St. Martin's Press, 1999. This volume in the "Let's Go" travel series is aimed at the budget-conscious traveler.

Rafael Steinberg and the Editors of Time-Life Books, *Pacific and Southeast Asian Cooking*. New York: Time-Life Books, 1970. This volume in Foods of the World series contains an appendix which describes the highlights of Australian and New Zealand cuisine.

PERIODICALS

Robert Hughes, "Fella Down a Hole," *Time,* July 5, 1999, p. 64.

Michael Parfit, "Australia—A Harsh Awakening," *National Geographic,* July 2000, pp. 2–31.

INTERNET SOURCES

Ted Anthony, "Sydney Olympic Games End," *AP Online,* October 2, 2000. special.northernlight.com/olympics/end.htm.

Amanda Hodge, "Act Now to Keep Your Cool," *The Australian,* July 20, 2001. www.theaustralian.news.com.au/common/story_page/0,5744,2515052%255E14769,00.html.

INDEX

Picture Credits

About the Author

John F. Grabowski is a native of Brooklyn, New York. He holds a bachelor's degree in psychology from City College of New York and a master's degree in educational psychology from Teacher's College, Columbia University. In addition to being a teacher for thirty-one years, he is a freelance writer, specializing in the fields of sports, education, and comedy. His body of published work includes thirty-four books; a nationally syndicated sports column; consultation on several math textbooks; articles for newspapers, magazines, and the programs of professional sports teams; and comedy material sold to Jay Leno, Joan Rivers, Yakov Smirnoff, and numerous other comics. He and his wife, Patricia, live in Staten Island with their daughter, Elizabeth.

DATE			

04 13(6) 20(7)

Illustrated by Caroline Davis

Written by Grace Swanton

This edition published by Parragon in 2008
Parragon
Queen Street House
4 Queen Street
Bath BA1 1HE, UK

Copyright © Parragon Books Ltd 2008

ISBN 978-1-4075-1706-3

Printed in China

I'm going to be the best ballerina ever!

PaRRagon

Bath · New York · Singapore · Hong Kong · Cologne · Delhi · Melbourne

One day I will go to ballet school.

I will learn how to dance.

I will wear ballet clothes.

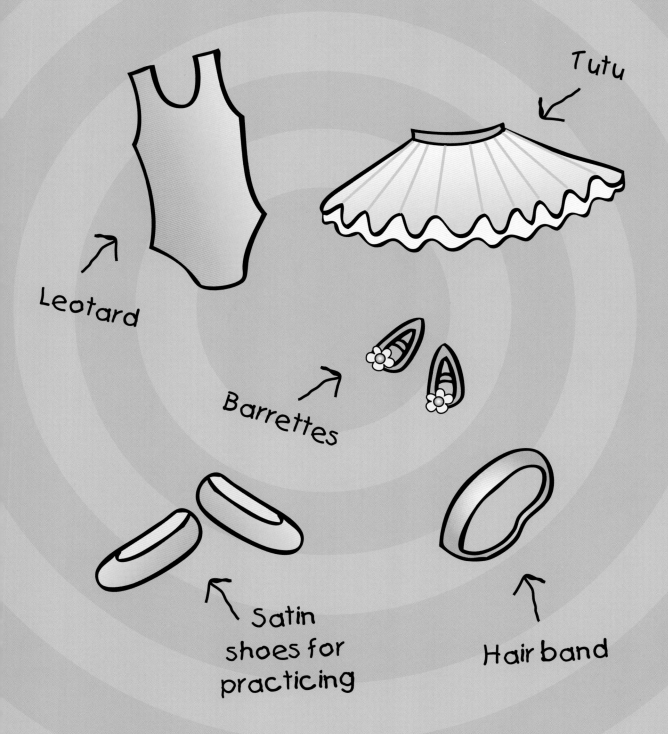

Tutu

Leotard

Barrettes

Satin shoes for practicing

Hair band

I will hold on to a bar when I practice.

Me in the mirror ←

Bar

I will point my toes really well. →

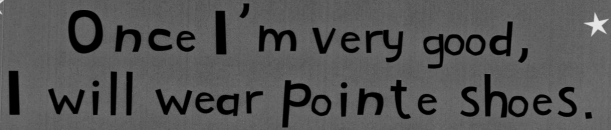

Once I'm very good,
I will wear Pointe shoes.

Pretty ribbons

There are hard pieces inside the ends of the toes.

Pointe shoes for dancing on tiptoe

I will reach up tall.

"I can touch the sky!"

I will be able to do the splits.

My amazing stretchy legs

I will jump up high . . .

"I'm a butterfly!"

. . . and bend down low.

This is called a plié. →

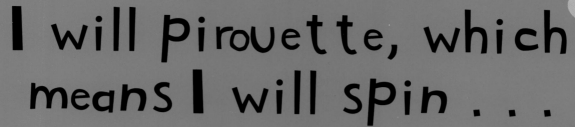

I will pirouette, which means I will spin . . .

around...

and around...

and around.

Wheeeeeeeeeeeeeee!

I will dance in a theater.

TONIGHT!
WORLD'S
BEST
BALLERINA

Me arriving
for my show

I will have a lot of costumes.

Very frilly tutu

Lots of sequins

Nobody else is allowed to wear this.

I will have my own dressing room backstage.

An assistant will do my hair and makeup.

A lot of people will come to watch me dance.

My grandpa

My mom

Everyone will clap and cheer my dancing.

They will give me a big, big bunch of flowers.

They will also throw flowers onto the stage.

Tired toes

I will travel all over the world to dance.

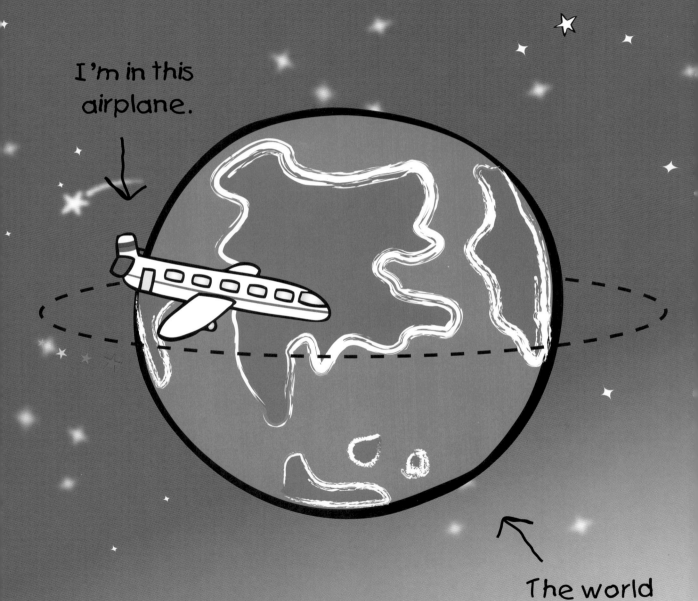

I'm in this airplane.

The world

I will be very famous and star in all the top ballets.

Me in Swan Lake.

Me in The Nutcracker.

That's me as Sleeping Beauty.

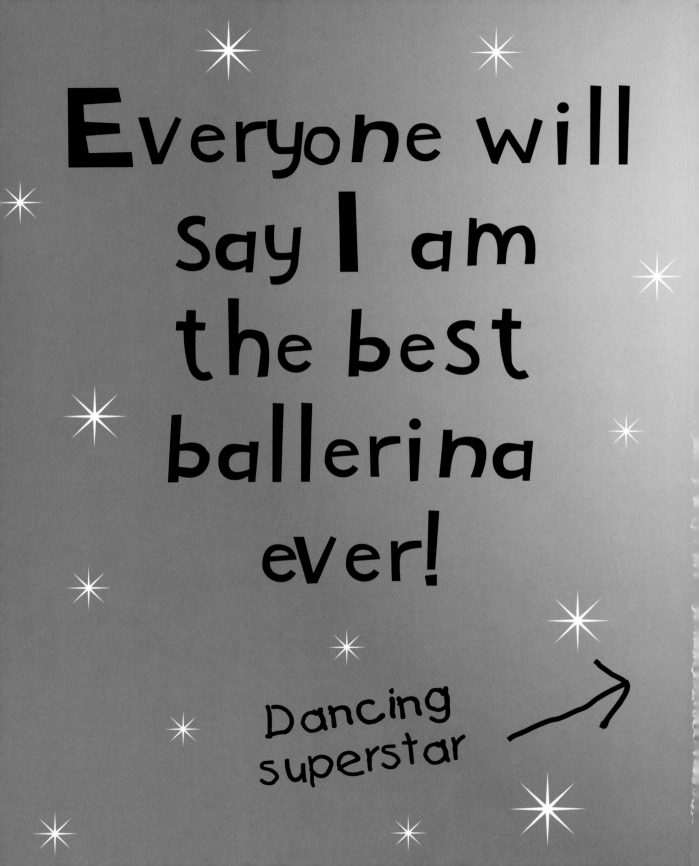

Everyone will say I am the best ballerina ever!

Dancing superstar →